ETTORE MAIOTTI
The Oil Painting Handbook

Learning from the Masters

Clarkson Potter/Publishers

Published in 1990 by Clarkson N. Potter, Inc., 201 East 50th Street, New York, NY 10022. Member of the Crown Publishing Group.
Originally published in Italy as Manuale pratico della pittura a olio.
First English language edition published in Great Britain by Aurum Press Ltd., in 1989.

Those drawings not otherwise cited are those of Ettore Maiotti.

CLARKSON N. POTTER, POTTER, and colophon are trademarks of Clarkson N. Potter, Inc.

Manufactured in Italy by Gruppo Editoriale Fabbri S.p.A., Milan

Library of Congress Cataloging - in - Publication Data

Maiotti, Ettore.
[Manuale pratico della pittura a olio. English]
The oil painting handbook: learning from the masters/by Ettore Maiotti.
p. cm.

1. Painting-Technique. I. Title.
ND 1500.M2413   1990
751.45-dc20   90-31522
                                                                                CIP

ISBN 0-517-57624-4
10 9 8 7 6 5 4 3 2 1

First American Edition

CONTENTS

INTRODUCTION

I came to oil painting rather late for an artist; I was twenty-four before I began to work in oils. Before that, I had studied fresco painting at the Art School of the Sforza Palace in Milan where Virginio Bertazzoni was teaching. To anyone unfamiliar with fresco painting, let me say that from a practical point of view, it must be the most demanding technique. Along with many other difficul-

ties and unlike oil painting, it does not allow for any mistakes. Michelangelo called oil painting 'women's painting' because in his day artists who corrected an error, changed a colour, or altered an expression that had already been decided upon in their preliminary sketches, were considered incompetent.

Influenced by Michelangelo's ideas and by my own studies, I had never paid much attention to oil painting. One day, however, I was given some oil paints as a present. Happily I have since overcome my prejudices and learned to appreciate the many possibilities of this technique. Once I began to study it (it had not even occurred to me when I was at art school), I discovered the depth of expression that one can achieve with oils, for they allow one to use colour in a multitude of ways, from the pale transparency of watercolours to the thick mass of colour that can be obtained with a palette knife.

The eagerness with which I approached this new technique was like an illness which I now call 'painting fever'. Be careful. It can strike you too. Here are its symptoms.

If, one day, you pass by an artists' suppliers and you see a handsome box of paints which you cannot resist buying in the window, or if you receive a gift of paints from a friend who knows of your interest, then one of two things can happen. You can either admire the paints for a moment and then carefully put them away in a drawer and forget about them, or you can try out your paints, probably unsuccessfully. In the latter case, you may begin to feel a certain dogged determination developing and enrol in a painting class. Or, if that is not possible, you may buy some books on the subject.

If you reach this stage, you have been bitten by the painting bug; the fever is in your bloodstream. Little by little, painting will become a source of endless fascination for you, one which can eventually take over and become your main reason for living. You will find yourself driven, constantly seeking new experiences and trying out new techniques. You will attend exhibitions and study the paintings, trying to work out how the artists achieved their effects and then go home inspired with new ideas. You will want to know how the painter used his brushes and which colours he preferred. You will delight in mixing colours on your own palette and obtaining a special colour you have seen in your mind's eye. A new and fascinating world will be opening up for you.

Please consider this book as a means of entering that world, a world I hope you will find full of wonder and surprises. Of course, there will be difficulties along the way and plenty of hard work. But it is a world that will give you back enough pleasure to make you forget the disappointments and exhaustion.

Ettore Maiotti

6

OIL PAINTS

An oil paint is composed of a pigment bound with a quick-drying oil. When exposed to air, the oil oxidizes to create a transparent elastic skin. With time, this skin increases in thickness on the surface of the canvas.

The binders most commonly used for oil paints are poppy oil, cold-pressed linseed oil and walnut oil.

Pigments or dyes are mixed and melted with clear, quick-drying, purified vegetable oils whose acidity should be carefully controlled. Certain shades are obtained by mixing pigments with cold-pressed linseed oil which has been filtered, rendered into a liquid and purified. Other colours, especially very light ones and white, are obtained by mixing pigments with poppy oil. Poppy oil, unlike linseed oil, does not cause paints mixed with it to yellow with age.

Even if you choose a binder carefully, however, it is impossible to avoid some yellowing of the surface if the canvas is left to dry in a dark place. To reduce drying time and minimize yellowing, I would advise you to leave your painting exposed to sunlight until it is completely dry. Then, hang it in a more protected area out of direct sunlight.

Media

Oil paints can be used squeezed directly from the tube or diluted with quick-drying oils or essential oils called media.

Quick-drying oils (cold-pressed linseed oil, poppy oil and walnut oil) result in a fluid paint and colours that retain their brilliance. With essential oils (distilled turpentine, not to be confused with other turpentines which are also extracts of pine resin but not distilled), the colours become more opaque. The characteristics of individual binders are:

Cold-pressed linseed oil: This form of linseed oil is the one most often used in painting. An extract of the flax plant (*Linum usitatissimum*), it is of Asiatic origin, pale and transparent in colour, and has a pleasant odour. It becomes lighter when it is left exposed to the sun in a transparent container.

Poppy oil: Much clearer than cold-pressed linseed oil and walnut oil, this is extracted from the seeds of the opium poppy (*Papaver somniferum*). It has the same characteristics as linseed oil but, because it is transparent by nature, it does not need to have colour removed. It is especially recommended for diluting light colours.

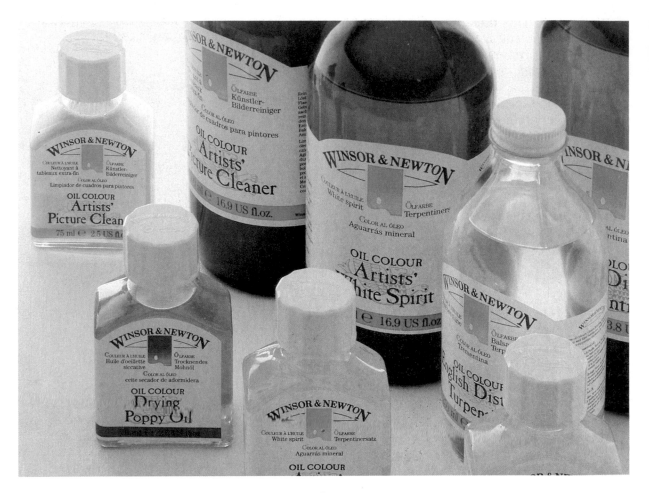

Walnut oil: This must have its colour removed by exposing it to light. In general, it has the same properties as linseed oil.

Essences and essential oils are volatile substances with a strong penetrating odour of either vegetable or mineral origin. Highly inflammable and soluble in alcohol, they should be used with great care.

When one dilutes a colour with one of these essences, a transparent colour is produced which is similar to watercolour.

In painting, the essences most often used are distilled turpentine and petroleum oils.

Distilled turpentine is an extract of resin from the pine (*Pinus*), larch (*Larix*) or other conifers. The larch furnishes most of the resins, and from it is produced Venice turpentine. Distilled turpentine yellows when exposed to the air and becomes oily; it cannot then be used for painting. It must, therefore, always be kept in an airtight bottle and a fresh amount should be made up each day.

Lavender oil, or oil of spike as it is more commonly called, is a slow-drying flammable liquid, which is preferred by artists who dislike the smell of turpentine.

White spirit (or turpentine substitute) is distilled from crude petroleum oils; it is an excellent medium which, unlike turpentine, gives the colour an opaque tone.

Pigments

Once you are familiar with oil binders and media, you can learn about colours.

Raw pigments are coloured substances that come in the form of fine dry powders which, once mixed with a binder, can be painted on to a support. When the pigment has been melted with a binder, it becomes a very solid resin. You may have noticed that after a few years oil tints which had barely been brushed on to the canvas have a luminosity and purity.

Pigments have traditionally been of either mineral, vegetable or animal origin, but today there are also very good synthetic pigments on the market.

The characteristics of some of the most common colours are given here.

Whites

Zinc white is obtained from an oxide of zinc. This pigment gives the most brilliant white of all, but it has comparatively poor covering power, and very slight steel-blue undertones. It mixes well with other colours, lightening them while retaining their brightness, and it does not darken from contact with hydrogen sulphide. It dries slowly and is non-toxic.

Silver white is a carbonate with a lead base. To stop it darkening over time, it should be mixed with zinc oxide. It will become darker if it comes into contact with hydrogen sulphide. As it is noxious, it should be handled with care.

Titanium white is a dioxide of titanium. A recently discovered pigment (it dates from the beginning of this century), it has begun increasingly to replace the other whites because of its excellent covering power.

Yellows

Chrome lemon is a pigment obtained from a lead chromate. It is a cool yellow that dirties the colour with which it is mixed. Mixed with silver white, it tends to darken.

Cadmium yellow is taken from cadmium sulphide, and many artists prefer it to the other yellows because it has no particular drawbacks. It mixes well with ultramarine blue to produce an intense shade of green, and is available in a range of tones from lemon yellow to orange.

Yellow ochre and mars yellow are taken from a hydrated ferric oxide and are more or

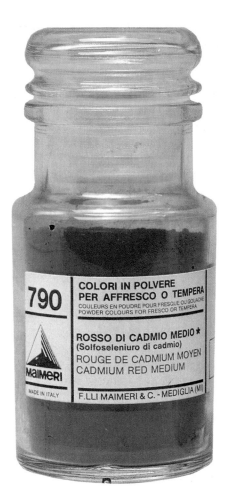

790

COLORI IN POLVERE
PER AFFRESCO O TEMPERA
COULEURS EN POUDRE POUR FRESQUE OU GOUACHE
POWDER COLOURS FOR FRESCO OR TEMPERA

ROSSO DI CADMIO MEDIO ★
(Solfoseleniuro di cadmio)
ROUGE DE CADMIUM MOYEN
CADMIUM RED MEDIUM

MAIMERI

MADE IN ITALY

F.LLI MAIMERI & C. - MEDIGLIA (MI)

less yellow depending on how much iron they contain.

Greens

Emerald green and viridian are obtained by heating an extract of hydrated chromium oxide. Transparent colours, they are weak in strength, but mixed with a little cadmium yellow become lovely bright greens. Viridian covers very well, unlike emerald green, but its colour – a slightly dull greyish-green – is less lively.

Cobalt green is a mixture of cobalt and zinc oxides and is available in several tones. It should not be mixed with any of the pigments that contain iron, like earth colours or ochres.

Reds

Carmine was made in the past from the desiccated bodies of the ladybird or cochineal beetle (*Cocus cacti*). It is a very pretty colour, but perhaps because of the high cost of producing it or because it was not very durable, it has been largely replaced by alizarin crimson or rose madder, extracted from the madder plant (*Rubia tinctorum*). Today carmine is extracted from aniline dyes. Mixed with blue, it gives marvellous violets and mixed with zinc white, brilliant pinks.

Cadmium red is a brilliant colour taken from cadmium sulpho-selenide and, as you might expect, it mixes well with the cadmium yellows. The amount of selenium it contains determines the precise colour tone which can range from orange to purple.

Scarlet vermilion is another extract now taken from aniline dyes. It has a brilliant tone and when mixed in small amounts with green produces an earthy colour. It is therefore useful for landscape painting. Its warm tone is incomparable. In the past it was extracted from mercuric sulphide and was very toxic; it is considered the oldest shade of red.

Blues

Cobalt blue is obtained through the calcination of cobalt salts with aluminium. It is a very bright pigment but has little covering power.

Prussian blue is a ferric ferrocyanide and difficult to find today. Mixed with cadmium yellow, it produces very pretty shades of green. Discovered around the middle of the eighteenth century, it has great covering power but it is not very light-fast.

Ultramarine is a polysulphide of sodium

which has replaced the old natural ultramarine blue made from grinding lapis lazuli into a fine powder. A beautiful brilliant blue, it produces lovely greens when mixed with cadmium yellow and, when mixed with carmine, it gives very brilliant violets.

Violets
Cobalt violet is a cobalt phosphate of weak covering power, but it is very light-resistant.

Browns
Browns range from raw sienna to burnt sienna, and from raw umber to burnt umber.

Blacks
Ivory black used to come from the oxidation of ivory. It has been replaced by a bone black, which comes from the oxidation of animal bones. It is a beautiful warm black but dries slowly.

Vine black is a vegetable carbon, obtained from vine branches which are then ground and sifted to obtain a bluish-black powder.

Organic Pigments
Organic pigments have an enormous variety of tones of great brilliance and, compared to non-organic pigments, high colouring power.

They run the gamut of colours and are obtained from petroleum-based chemicals. Organic pigments fall into a small number of chemical categories, which are:

Aniline dyes ('Azos'), ranging in shade from yellows to reds and clarets.

Anthracene derives from coal tar, and covers a range from yellows to reds and blues.

Copper phthalocyanine pigments are very light-resistant blues and greens which can replace non-organic colours in brilliance.

Quinacridone pigments range from pink to red to violet. They include colours that do not exist as non-organic colours.

Dioxazines are very light-resistant pigments that cover the range of violets beyond the quinacridones.

The properties of each pigment are written on the tube of paint. The degree of permanence or light-fastness for each pigment may be indicated as 'extremely permanent', 'durable', 'moderately durable' or 'fugitive', or by a series of stars (one star for the most fugitive colours, four stars for extremely permanent colours), or by a system of letters (AA for 'extremely permanent', then A for 'durable', B for 'moderately durable' and C for 'fugitive').

Some tubes also indicate the degree of transparency of the pigment, marking it either with a simple symbol such as a *, or labelling it 'opaque', 'semi-opaque', 'semi-transparent', or 'transparent'.

Colours that are labelled toxic should be used with care since they can be harmful if they come into contact with the skin or if they are swallowed. Certain pigments used in the past, either because they are no longer available, or because they are noxious, or are not light-resistant enough, have been re-placed, as can be seen in the table below, by more stable non-toxic products with constant and pure tones.

One of the main problems with pigments is their sensitivity to light. To increase the life of your painting, do not leave it hanging in direct sunlight once it has dried; store it as soon as possible in a more protected place. For a graphic example of what happens when paints are left exposed to sunlight, look at the two colour tables on the following page.

Name	Original Pigment	Reason for Discontinuance	New Pigment
Saturn red	Imitation lead oxide	Very noxious, unstable	Perinone orange, quinacridone
Imitation Indian yellow	Indian yellow	Not available	Aniline dye, perinone orange
Naples yellow light	Lead antimoniate	Noxious, unstable	Oxides of zinc, iron, sulphur, cadmium
Naples yellow dark	Lead antimoniate	Noxious, unstable	Oxides of zinc, iron, sulphur, cadmium sulpho-selenide
Naples yellow red	Lead antimoniate	Noxious, unstable	Oxides of zinc, sulphur, cadmium (sulpho-selenide)
Imitation gamboge	Gamboge	Unavailable, noxious	Aniline dyes
Veronese green	Acetyl-arsenate of copper	Toxic, unstable	Aniline dyes, phthalocyanine of chloride, zinc oxide

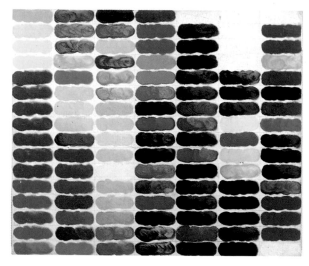

Colours not exposed to the sun.

Colours left exposed to direct sunlight for a year.

Supports

The supports most often used for oil painting are unbleached linen and cotton duck canvases (synthetic materials are not suitable for oil paint). When properly prepared, linen and cotton canvases can also be used for large-format paintings. These canvases can be purchased already stretched and prepared but it is always better for the painter to carry out these steps himself. It is of fundamental importance to the success of a painting to know how to prepare a canvas. Preparation affects not only the durability of the painting itself but also its stability and the ease with which the surface takes the paint.

Besides canvas, wood, cardboard and hardboard can also be used as supports.

Glue Sizing

Because of its resistance to water and humidity, casein glue (also known as milk glue) is often used to prepare the canvas.

14

Rabbit-skin glue is also commonly used. Both are available from artists' suppliers in powder form or as granules.

Grounds

A ground is used to create a surface that will take paint; it also forms a barrier between the paint and the support, thereby preserving and protecting the support. French chalk, also called Paris white or whiting, is a particularly good ground made from crushed calcium carbonate. When mixed with a binder and pigment and compressed, this can be made into pastel crayons.

Gilder's whiting is sold as a powder or in small chunks (which become crumbly in water). Mixed with linseed oil, this forms a putty that will stay soft for a long time; it is often used when replacing windowpanes.

Kaolin or China clay can also be used as long as it is mixed with another ground. On its own, it has a tendency to crumble.

Preparing Canvas, Wood and Cardboard

There are many ways to prepare supports but I will limit myself to three recipes chosen for their simplicity. If you are interested in more, I suggest you search out nineteenth-century handbooks for artists.

Recipe One

This is best prepared the night before you intend to use it.

Soak four handfuls of rabbit-skin glue in half a litre (20 fl. oz.) of cold water for twelve hours in a metal container. You will notice that the granules of glue swell up but remain separate from one another. If the glue dissolves completely in the water, it means it is of poor quality and you should look for another kind.

After soaking it the required length of time, put the container inside a larger heat-proof container and fill the gap with boiling water. Then place it over a low heat to warm the glue.

After a few minutes, check to see whether the glue is ready. To test it, pick up a small amount between your thumb and index finger and see how sticky it is. If it is very sticky, add a little hot water; if it is not sticky enough, add more granules. It should be rather thick.

Mix together equal measures of French chalk or whiting and China clay, add the same measure of glue, and half as much of linseed oil. Blend all this together and then with a large flat hair-type brush, spread the mixture over your canvas or wood.

This mixture will not keep. Once it is cold it becomes hard and after twenty-four hours it decomposes.

Recipe Two
This does not make as white a ground as the first recipe. You will need two parts French chalk or whiting and one part grey clay (available from artists' suppliers). The dried clay should be ground. Add water to the clay and chalk until it becomes a semi-liquid paste, then add an equal amount of rabbit-skin glue prepared according to the first recipe. The glue should be warm when you add it. If the mixture does not blend well, heat it a little longer. If it is not sticky enough, add more glue; to make it more fluid, add a little linseed oil.

Recipe Three
If you want a darker background for your support, try this recipe.

Soak 20 grams ($\frac{3}{4}$ oz.) of casein in a glass container with 60 millilitres (2 fl. oz.) of cold water. Leave it for about twenty minutes then stir it with a piece of wood. Do not let the casein come into contact with metal. Next, add 4 grams (a few drops) of ammoniac, stirring constantly, until you have a homogeneous mixture. Add a tablespoon of glycerine, mix again, then strain it through cheesecloth or muslin. Spread a coat of casein glue over the canvas and let it dry.

Meanwhile, mix 10 parts zinc white to one or two parts vine black (depending on how dark you want it). Add this to the glue in equal portions, one part pigment to one part glue, blend it all together well and spread the mixture over your canvas.

Stretchers
Stretcher frames can be any shape you want, but the most common frames, however, are rectangular and are made of four strips of wood fitted together at the corners by a system of tenon and mortise joints.

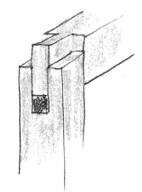

If the frame is small, these four strips of wood are enough, but if they are longer than one metre (3 ft), insert a crosspiece or batten to avoid any distortion of the frame.

A good-quality stretcher frame will also have eight keys or small wedges, two for each corner, to help keep the frame square when the painting is finished. These keys or wedges should be gently tapped into place with a hammer to keep the canvas taut.

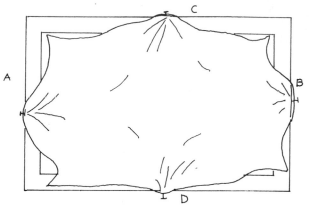

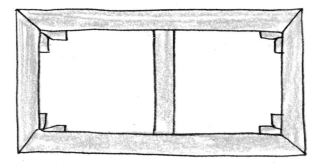

Soaking and Stretching the Canvas

To attach the canvas to the frame, first soak the fabric in water, then place it, still wet, on the frame as shown above. The first nail or staple (if you have a heavy-duty stapler) should be pounded in at point A, in the

middle of one of the shorter sides of the frame. Now, holding the canvas with your

hand or using canvas pliers (like the pair in the photo), stretch it to point B and attach it to the frame as you did at point A. Continue around the frame, attaching the canvas at points C and D. Then staple or nail the cor-

18

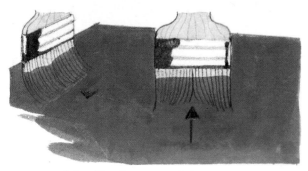

ners and finally the rest of the canvas, trying to space the staples evenly around the edge. Try to work quickly – the whole process should be finished before the canvas dries.

Next, spread your ground over the canvas with a large flat bristle brush. I suggest a No. 12 which is good for both large and small canvases. Place the canvas on a flat surface (or on the floor if it is very big). To spread the mixture correctly, brush down the length of the canvas first, then go back over it, crosswise, re-soaking your brush as necessary. Finish by going over the canvas in both directions with a dry brush to be sure the ground is evenly spread.

Some Advice

If, for any reason, the canvas ends up with wrinkles, soak the reverse side of the fabric with hot water. When it dries, it should be flat.

To repair a tear, use a razor blade to cut off the frayed edge, then place the canvas on a table, wrong side up. Wet the area around the tear. Take a piece of linen that is lighter in weight than your canvas and glue it over the tear with the same glue you used for the ground (rabbit-skin glue or casein). Let it dry, then turn it over and clean it with a cottonbud dipped in warm water. If the repaired area is very uneven, fill it in with a little oil paint of the same shade as the background and smooth it down with a palette knife.

Preparing a Wood Support

You prepare wood in the same basic way as you prepare canvas. If you want a chalkier ground (if you were painting a mural panel, for instance), add twenty per cent chalk to your mixture.

The best woods for oil painting are plywoods and smooth natural woods without woodworm or knots. Avoid pressed woods. All wood should have been previously ex-

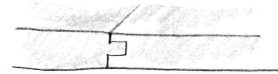

posed to water and sunlight so that it will not crack or warp later.

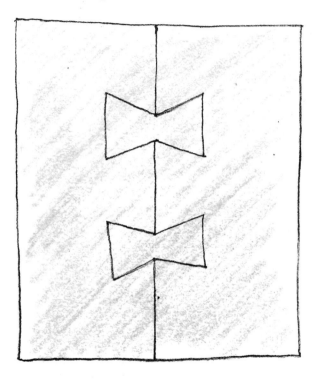

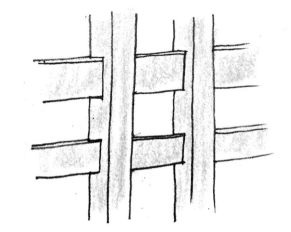

can use metal reinforcements.

Preparing Cardboard
Cardboard is also prepared like canvas, except that both sides should be coated so that when the ground dries, the cardboard does not buckle.

Canvas, wood, cardboard – wood and cardboard especially – can also be used directly without any special preparation, with varying results. Toulouse-Lautrec worked mostly on grey untreated cardboard.

The boards should be put together as shown in the drawing and then reinforced with dovetail joints. If the board is large, you

Brushes

Until the middle of the nineteenth century, artists made their own brushes, tailored to their needs. Only in the second half of that century did specialist craftsmen start to manufacture and sell artists' brushes. Today, although there are whole industries dedicated to making them, artists' paintbrushes are still made in a craftsmanlike way.

The selection of hair or bristles and the preparation of the tip are carried out by people with years of experience. They know by touch how to evaluate the amount of hair to use, how to position the tips in the right direction and how to give each brush the shape and size required.

Besides the hair, the handle and ferrule (or metal grip) of the brush must be chosen with care.

Most brushes are made from hog's hair, ox-hair, sable, squirrel hair or a synthetic fibre. Bristles are less supple and more resistant than hair, so a bristle brush is very good for working with oil paints. Also, the tips retain a greater amount of paint. They come with the following regular tips: round, flat, and filbert, which is between round and flat. Fan-shaped brushes are also available – these are useful for blending colours together.

Bristle Brushes

The bristles used for these brushes are taken from the back of the hog or boar. Today most bristles come from China and are made from bleached hog's hair. The principal characteristic of a bristle brush is its ability to hold the paint and spread it evenly over the canvas. This is why it is so often used for oil painting.

Sable Brushes

Kolinsky hair brushes which come from the Siberian or Manchurian sable are the best, but expensive. They are extremely hardy and very elastic, with a long, supple and very resilient tip. They are the best brushes for watercolours, touch-ups and fine work.

Ox-hair Brushes

These brushes are made from the light-coloured hair from the ears of oxen. They are very resilient, but somewhat clumsy, so not as well suited for precise work. They are most suitable when a fine hand is not necessary.

Squirrel-hair Brushes

Though these brushes are very silky, they do not have the same elasticity as those made from sable hair. Their strong point is that they are much less expensive than other brushes and so are largely used by school-children and for large watercolour brushes.

Synthetic-fibre Brushes

These are also used today for oil painting. They have a very good tip but they do not hold the paint as well as sable hair brushes and they are not as resilient. They can be cleaned easily and frequently without harm.

They are particularly suitable for colours that dry quickly, such as acrylics.

A Curious Fact

I said earlier that painters and decorators in the past made their own brushes. Very often painters would buy old brushes from decorative artists (not to be confused with today's house painters) because these brushes had already been 'broken in'. The brushes would then be thoroughly cleaned and taken apart. The fine supple hair would be cut to the length the artist required for the new brush and used again.

The Ferrule

The ferrule (or metal grip) should be strong, resistant to corrosion and staining, and seamless. The ferrules of good brushes are usually made of nickel or cupro-nickel. The most economical brushes have aluminium ferrules.

The shape and diameter of the ferrule determines the shape of the bristles. The brush is sized according to the fullness of its head.

The Handle

The perfect handle is one of ideal weight, well-balanced, and easily manipulated.

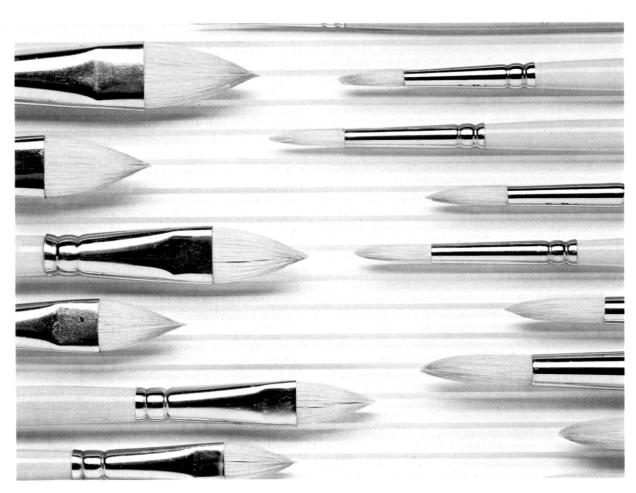

24

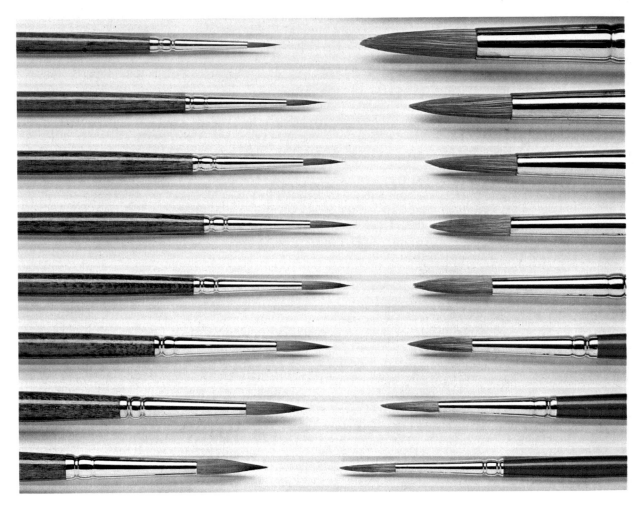

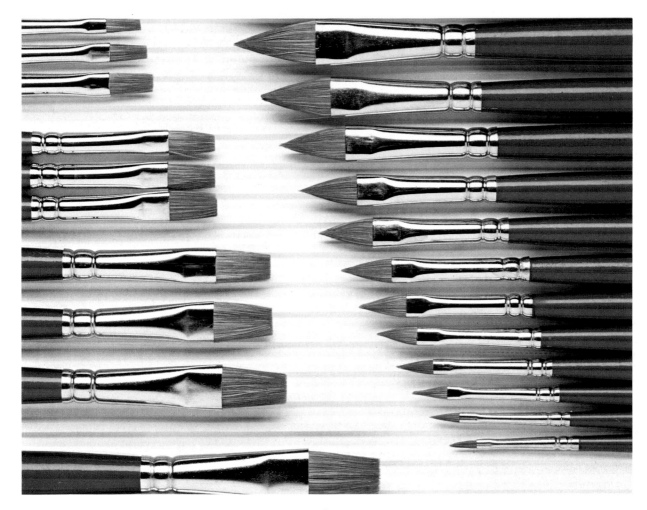

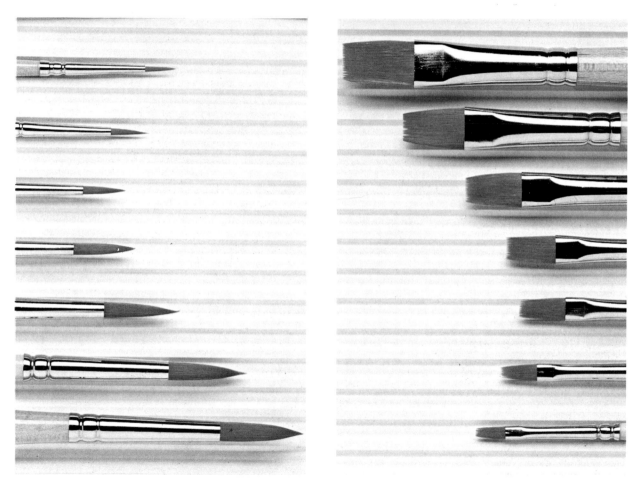

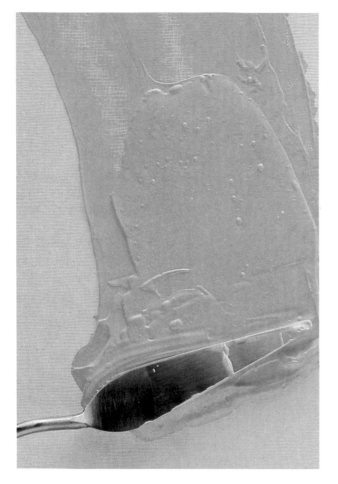

Its size depends on its length and also on how long it will be used.

Caring for Your Brushes

It is important to take care of brushes if they are to last a long time. Rinse them as soon as possible after use, then wash them with soap and water, and dry them carefully.

If the paint dries before you can clean the brush, use turpentine or white spirit to soften the paint, then rinse the brush in water. Re-shape the points with your fingers and store the brushes upright, bristle end up.

Palette Knives

The palette knife is a flexible stainless-steel tool with a wooden handle, used to mix colours with a binder or to mix two colours together, before spreading them on your canvas. It is also a good tool with which to clean your palette. There are two kinds of palette knife, one with a broad rounded blade like a knife, and the other with a small angular blade like a trowel.

Brush-holders

These are little cups that have a metal spiral suspended above them. You can fix your brush to the spiral and leave it to soak in turpentine in the cup without letting the tips of the bristles rest on the bottom of the cup.

These are very useful for the absent-minded painter who tends to forget his brushes, leaving them standing in a jar and damaging them irreparably. Since his brushes are the painter's basic tools, it is important to treat them well.

Dippers

These little metallic cups, with or without lids, clip on to the side of the palette and can hold either turpentine or oil.

They are very useful, especially for the first stage of a landscape painting.

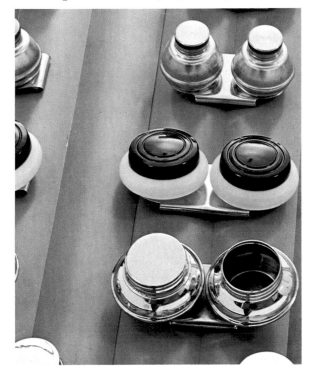

The Palette

The palette is such an important element for the painter that I will discuss it at length. Just as a good draughtsman can be measured by how well he sharpens his pencils, so the measure of a good colourist is the way he arranges his paints on his palette. It does not matter what material the palette is made from as long as it allows you to gather together and arrange your paints on it. Plywood is often used because it is light and practical. Palettes come in two standard shapes, oval and rectangular, but, of course, you can have one made in any shape you like.

Clean your palette as soon as you finish your work. Usually most of the paint can be scraped off with a knife. If you do leave it and the paint dries, try the following method of removing the old paint. Outdoors, where there is no danger of fire, pour a small amount of turpentine over the dried paint. Set the bottle of turpentine aside some distance away (because it is highly flammable), then light the surface of the palette. The heat will soften the paint and make it more liquid (take care that the fire does not burn the wood of the palette). When the paint is soft, put out the fire and scrape the surface with your palette knife. As the palette cools, the paint will become hard again, so you must work quickly.

Colour Theory

From now on, when I refer to the palette, I will not be talking about the wooden board described on the previous page, but about the ensemble of colours arranged on it.

The palette is never an improvisation; it follows very precise rules. All painters arrange their colours following a fixed pattern. At least, that is the way painters did it in the past. Today, there are different attitudes to colour theory, with rules that seem quite rigid to me. However, none of these theories is able to create a palette as luminous and bright as the one used by the Impressionists. Recently, I came across a new method whereby the student should fill his notebook with the different ranges of colours. This practice, widely used today, may make the work of the teacher easier but it does not teach the student much, for he does not learn to reflect on colours. In fact, instead of learning to recognize the colours of objects so that he can then interpret them and transfer them on to a canvas, the student falls into the trap of depending on strict rules which leave him no room for free expression.

In the nineteenth century, scientific interest in colour theory was reflected in the painter's palette. But scientific theory was only a tool employed by painters who then interpreted it and applied it according to rules of their own; they did not all conform to the same ones.

You may find it interesting to know what Eugène Delacroix thought about colour as he expressed it in the 'Journal' he kept for most of his life. In this entry, he tries to explain how one goes about painting shiny objects and how the three basic colours are used to portray shadows and reflections:

'The law about using green for reflections and along the edges of shadows and violet for the cast shadow, which I discovered earlier with linen, can be extended to everything, just as you can find the three colours mixed in everything. I had previously thought that they were only present in some things.

'With the sea, this is quite plain. The projected shadows are clearly violet and the reflections are, also, quite clearly green.

'Here again we find that nature's laws are consistent. Just as a drawing is made up of many smaller drawings and a wave is

made of smaller waves, so, in the same way, daylight is divided or broken down into parts. The most obvious law about this breaking down of things is the one that first struck me as being the most general, that regarding the sheen of an object. The kind of object in which I have most often noticed the presence of the three tones together are: a piece of armour, a diamond, and so on. One finds them in other objects too, certain fabrics and linen for example, certain effects of landscapes, and above all, the sea, where this effect is also very marked. It was not long before I realized that this effect is particularly striking with flesh. Now I have become convinced that nothing exists without these three tones. So then, when I find linen with a violet shadow and a green reflection, does it mean that it has only two tones? Is it not inevitable that orange is also there because of the yellow found in green and the red contained in violet?

'Explore more deeply the law which, in shiny fabrics, and especially satin, places the true colour of the object next to its sheen – another example would be a horse's hide.

'I notice a wall made of very red bricks in a little winding street. The part that is exposed to the sun is orangish-red, the shadow very violet, brownish-red, Cassel earth and white.

'For light colours, the non-reflecting shadow must be made rather violet and it should be reflected with rather greenish tones. There is a red flag outside my window. And indeed, its shadow seems to be a matt violet. The transparency seems orangish, but why is there no green found here? First of all, because of the need for the red to have green shadows but also because of the presence of orange and violet, two tones in which yellow and blue are found, which in turn give green.

'The true tone of the skin, that is, the tone least broken down, should be the one closest to the object with a sheen, i.e., silken fabrics, a horse's hide, etc. As flesh has a rather matt surface, the same thing happens to it as happens with objects in sunlight, where the contrasts are more obvious.

'One day, I worked out that linen always has a green reflection and a violet shadow.

'I perceive that the sea follows the same pattern, the difference being that the reflection is modified because of the important role the sky plays, since, with cast shadows, the sea is clearly violet.

'It is very likely that I will discover that

this law holds true for everything. Shadows on land, no matter what it is that casts them, are violet. I can see from my window the shadows of people passing by on the sand. The sand, by itself, is violet, but in the sun it appears golden; this is because the shadows cast by these people are so violet that, in contrast, the ground becomes yellow.

'And would it be too much to say that outside, the reflection must be derived from the yellow ground gilded by the sun and the blue sky, and that these two colours necessarily produce green? Obviously, in sunlight, one has seen these effects revealed quite clearly, but even when the sunlight disappears, the relationship among these colours should remain the same. In other words, if the ground looks less golden because there is less sunlight, the reflection will also look less green and less vigorous. I had always made my linen true in tone. Now I discover that the shadow is violet and the reflection green.

'These are documents of which even a scholar could be proud; I am all the more so for having done paintings correctly before I was aware of these laws.'

In a letter which Vincent van Gogh wrote to his brother Théo, we find more fresh ideas.

'I received your letter and its contents yesterday. What you say about a certain study of a small basket with some apples is interesting, but did you think it up yourself??? Because, if my memory serves me well, that's not the way you used to see things. No matter, it puts us back on the road to agreeing about colour. Keep studying these questions for they will carry you on a long way. Burger and Mantz and Silvestre know about such things as this. Let me explain simply how this study was made. Green and red are complementary colours. Now then, there is a certain shade of red in the apples that by itself is rather vulgar, and next to it, there are some greenish things. And there are also one or two apples of another colour, a certain shade of pink that gives the whole affair value; this pink is the colour broken down from mixing the red that I mentioned and the green.

'That is why there is a harmony between the colours. There is a second contrast thrown in: that of the background with the foreground. One is a neutral colour, obtained from blue broken by orange; the other is the same neutral colour but modified by adding a little yellow to it.

'One of the studies seemed to you a variation on the theme of grey-brown, and it's true, that was the case; in fact, they all were – those with the potatoes, that is – with the difference that one is a study of raw sienna, the other of burnt sienna and the third yellow ochre and red ochre.

'The last one and the one most important to me is, I think, the best, in spite of the matt black background which I left matt on purpose because the ochres are also not naturally transparent colours. Speaking of this study, the biggest potato was done by modifying the non-transparent ochres, breaking them down with a transparent blue.

'The red ochre with the yellow ochre forms orange, their combination with blue becomes more neutral and next to this neutralized colour, they seem either redder or more yellow. The lightest spot in the whole canvas is just a little pure yellow ochre. And the fact that the matt yellow is still more or less apparent is because it is in quite a neutral area that is violet in colour; red ochre with blue is good with the violet tones.

'The birds' nests are also painted on a black background and this was done purposely because in these studies I wanted to express openly that these objects are not found in their natural setting but in a con-trived background. In nature, a nest looks quite different; one doesn't see much of the nest, one mostly sees the birds in it.

'When you want to paint nests taken from your own collection, you do not want to draw too much attention to the fact that in nature the background and the setting are completely different. I have therefore made the background black. A coloured background is more attractive in a still-life. In Amsterdam I saw some still-lifes painted by Mlle Voss that I thought were excellent, much more beautiful than those by Blaise Desgoffe, truly worthy of Beyeren. And it occurred to me that the calm still-lifes of that woman painter had more artistic value than many of the pretentious canvases by other painters in Amsterdam.

'I will send you the book by Blanc; please order for me as soon as possible the Art of the 18th Century that I may read it. I especially want to read Goncourt's piece about Chardin.

'Lacase's Rembrandt also truly has the feeling of Rembrandt's last period; it's been twelve years since I saw it but I still remember how much it struck me, as much as that head by Fabritius in Rotterdam. If I remember correctly, that female nude of the

Lacase Collection is also very pretty and from the last period as well. The fragment of "The Anatomy Lesson" by Rembrandt was also a great surprise. Do you remember the flesh tones? They were earth-coloured, especially the feet.

'There is also sometimes – in fact, I would say always – a relationship of opposites between the tone of the garment and that of the face.

'Red and green are contrasting colours; "The Singer" from the Dupper Collection, which has carmine tones in the skin colour, has green tones in the black sleeves and a different red from the carmine in the little bows on the sleeves.

'The orange, blue and white figure, which I wrote to you about, has a relatively neutral coloured face, a slightly earthy pink, somewhat purplish, in contrast to the outfit of yellow leather à la Frans Hals.

'Cheery citron yellow cools to a matt violet in the cheeks. Now then! the darker the garment, the paler the face; this does not happen by chance; at least in this portrait and that of the woman in the garden, there are two black violets (blue violet and red violet) and a single black (yellow black?); I repeat: red violet and blue violet, black and black, the three most sombre colours. And the faces are extraordinarily pale, even for Hals.

'But tell me, regarding black and white, is one allowed to use them or not? Are they forbidden fruit?

'I don't think so. Frans Hals had twenty-seven different blacks.

'As for white, you know yourself that some characteristic canvases have been painted, precisely and on purpose, by modern colourists, using white on white. What does it mean then to say one cannot use them? Delacroix called black and white "restful".

Any colour can be used as long as it is employed properly and its relationship to other colours taken into account.

'No, black and white have their uses and their meanings and avoiding them will not work. To consider them both as neutral tones makes much more sense; white: the maximum combination of the lightest shades of red, of blue and of yellow; and black: the maximum combination of the darkest tones of red, blue and yellow.

'Against such an argument I have nothing to say, I find it completely justified. So! Light or dark, the tone, as far as value is concerned, lies in that fourth range of black and white.

Is it not true that one has

Scale 1:	Yellow	Violet
Scale 2:	Red	Green
Scale 3:	Blue	Orange
Total	--	
A fourth scale (that of neutral colours, made of red+blue+ yellow)	White (red+blue +yellow, at the lightest end)	Black (red+blue +yellow, at the darkest end)

'This is how I see blacks and whites. If I mix red and green together to make a greenish-red or a reddish-green, I get, by adding white, a greenish-pink or a pinkish-green. And if you like, by adding black, a greenish-brown or a brownish-green. Isn't that easy enough to understand?

'If I mix some yellow and some violet together to try to get a yellowish-lilac or a lilac-yellow, in other words, a neutralized yellow or a neutralized violet, I get grey by adding white or black. That is, greys and browns. This is most important when one is making lighter or darker colours, whether their nature be red, yellow or blue.

'To speak of light or dark greys and browns expresses it well. But what Sylvestre said of Delacroix is nice: that he took a colour, some unnameable nuance, from his palette by chance, then he placed this colour somewhere, either with the most luminous light colours or the darkest shadows, and he made of that sludge something that was either as bright as light or as dark as the deepest shadows.

'I once heard of an experiment done with a neutral-coloured piece of paper. It appeared greenish on a red background, reddish on a green ground, bluish on an orange ground, yellowish on a violet ground and violet on a yellowish one.

'Listen, Theo, imagine that you are trying to make a muddy colour look clear on a canvas, trying to do what Delacroix said of Veronese – even with a colour like mud, Veronese was able to paint a blonde female nude so that the woman looked blonde and white in the painting. Now how is it possible without the opposition of great strengths of blue-black or blue-violet or brown-red-blue?

'You look at paintings and note their dark shadows, you think that when shadows are dark, and I mean by that, black, that they are not worth anything. But are you right?

'I don't think so, for then "Dante" by Delacroix, for example, or "The Fisherman" by Zandvoort is not worth anything either because one finds there the greatest and most solid shades of blue-blacks and violet-blacks. Didn't Rembrandt and Hals use black? And Velàsquez??? And not only black, but twenty-seven different blacks, I can assure you. So, when you say 'don't use black', are you sure you know what you are saying? Think it over, because frankly, for you to come to this conclusion, there are only two possibilities: either you learned and understood the question of tones wrongly or you had only a vague idea of it to begin with which you didn't fully understand. There are many who think like you! Even among the great. But through the example of Delacroix and others of his era, you will end up by coming round. And by the way, haven't you noticed in some of my studies that the dark backgrounds are very muted in their light zones?

'And that, where I use colours more muted than in nature (since my colours are more sombre not only in the shadows but also, relatively, in the areas of light), I at least respect the relationship between tones? My studies are done as precisely as a gymnast when I raise and lower my tones.'

After years of studying painting and with long experience of the techniques of colour printing, I have tried to synthesize the different aspects of my knowledge into a system. This system takes account of scientific principles but is also aware of the poetic rapport between the colours of objects that one perceives and interprets on canvas.

Primary, Secondary and Complementary Colours

The three basic colours, from which all the other colours are derived, are cyan blue, yellow and magenta red. These are referred to as *primary colours*.

Arrange them as shown in figure 1 so that each one is at one of the points of an equilateral triangle which is then enclosed within a circle.

If you mix equal parts of yellow and blue, you get green, mixing blue and red produces violet, and mixing yellow and red gives orange.

These colours are called *secondary colours*.

Now draw another equilateral triangle inside the same circle and place the secondary colours, green, orange and violet, at the points of the second triangle so that each

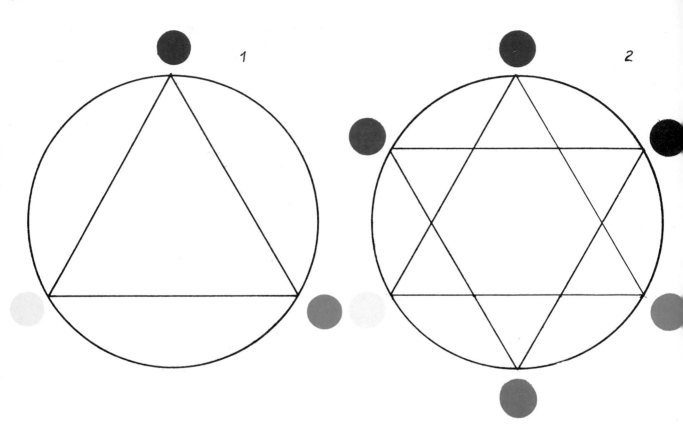

one is between the two primary colours that constitute them. You now have a colour star. Note that green lies opposite red, its *complementary colour*. In the same way, yellow

is the complement of violet, and orange is the complement of blue (figure 2). In the range of colours available to artists, cyan, magenta and yellow will not be as pure as the colours used in printing, so the colours derived from them will not be as pure.

From now on, to simplify things, we will use ultramarine for blue, carmine for red and cadmium yellow for yellow.

These create very suitable secondary colours. Using them, you can arrange a very brilliant palette such as the Impressionists or Pointillists had. To do this, follow the exercises here, which I worked out using oil paint diluted with turpentine and No. 0 hard bristle brushes with a flat tip.

Draw an equilateral triangle and fill it in with ultramarine blue.

Draw another triangle, point down, and fill it in with light cadmium yellow.

Draw the two triangles superimposed one over the other. The overlapping part will be green, which comes from mixing equal parts of blue and yellow.

The green that you obtain from the blue and yellow should be very balanced, neither too blue nor too yellow. If the green is too blue, add a little yellow, and vice-versa.

Repeat the same exercise with carmine and ultramarine and you get violet. If it is too dark, add a touch of white.

Do the exercise again, this time using carmine and cadmium yellow to get orange.

Notice that you are working with only three colours (red, blue and yellow).

Red + blue = violet; yellow, the colour not used, is the complementary colour.

Red + yellow = orange; blue, which is not used, is its complementary colour.

Yellow + blue = green; red is the complementary colour.

Violet, blue and green are cool colours; red, yellow and orange are warm colours.

Mix equal parts of violet, which you have made with red and blue, and yellow: you will get bistre (a very dark, grey colour).

You will also get bistre by mixing blue with orange, and green with red. These shades of bistre can be used to darken colours.

Do not try to make colours darker by using a shade of black. This is a serious error: you will only produce dirty muted colours with no life or brilliance to them, with no 'music'.

Add a little white to bistre and you will get

a bright neutral grey; if the grey is too warm, add a little blue; if it is greenish, add red and if it is too violet, add yellow.

All colours can be made warm or cool.

Draw nine squares side by side, fill in the fifth or middle one with carmine and designate it '0'. Now fill in the four squares to the left of it with red, gradually adding more yellow as you move farther away from '0'. Next, fill in the squares on the right with red to which you gradually add more blue. You will notice that all the reds to the left of '0' are warmer than it is, and that those to the right of '0' are cooler.

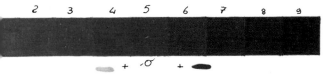

Repeat this exercise using yellow as your base colour and adding red to the squares as you move left, and blue as you fill in the squares on the right.

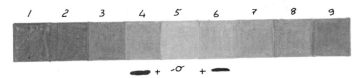

Now use blue, with red added to the squares on the left and yellow to those on the right.

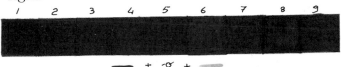

If you have methodically added more colour to your base each time, you will create the illusion of a staircase, going up from the left to the centre and down from the centre to the right. As you mix your colours, follow the examples above as closely as you can. To finish the exercise, progressively add more white and you will get a range of pale tones.

To train your eye to see the warm and cool shades of a colour, look, for example, at the leaves of a tree. At first, you will see nothing but an enormous mass of green, but gradually you will begin to notice that in some places the green is lighter and in others, darker; in some parts, it is warmer and in others, cooler. And if the tree is near a house with a red roof, it will take on a light, almost imperceptible, red reflection.

Continue this exercise by again colouring the yellow and blue triangles. Join their points together to form a hexagon and fill in the spaces with carmine, the complementary colour of green. Use the sides of the hexagon to form six more triangles and you will have another star. Fill in the new triangles with a shade that is six parts green and one

part red.

Now join the points and you will have formed a new hexagon; fill in the spaces with carmine. Draw another star and fill it in with green (six parts) mixed with red (two parts). Continue on in this manner, mixing green and red, until you have reached a mix of six parts green with six parts red.

You should also try this exercise with a base of red and blue, to which you add yellow, and red and yellow, then blue.

Now let us try a series of exercises with earth colours.

Earth colours are those that are mixed with earth: raw sienna, raw umber, burnt sienna and burnt umber.

To create these colours, proceed as follows: to nine parts of cadmium yellow, add one part raw sienna, then carefully mix them, diluting them as usual.

Do the same with ultramarine and burnt sienna.

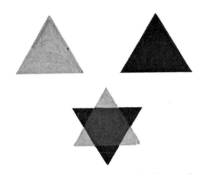

Now repeat the exercise with the coloured triangles and you will obtain an earth shade of green.

If you substitute raw umber for the raw sienna, you will obtain a different shade of earth green. Using the same proportions,

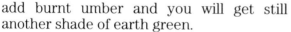

add burnt umber and you will get still another shade of earth green.

Do the same exercise with red and blue and the earth tones, and then with yellow and red plus the earth tones.

Now, let's experiment with some optical illusions produced with colour.

If you look at the white dot in the centre of the red square for about two minutes and then you turn your gaze to the black dot on the white square, you will see the complementary colour of red appear as a halo.

This will happen with the other colours; try this with neon lights in the cinema, in shops and signs and with *silhouettes*.

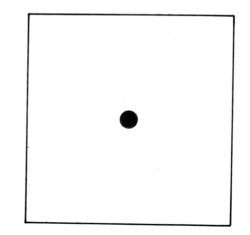

Arranging Colours on Your Palette

Now we will begin the true work of the painter by arranging our colours on the palette.

First you must prepare a fixed scale of col-our values and arrange them around your palette as follows: yellow ochre, cadmium yellow light, dark cadmium yellow, vermilion, carmine, burnt sienna, burnt umber, Vandyke brown, indigo, ultramarine, ceru-

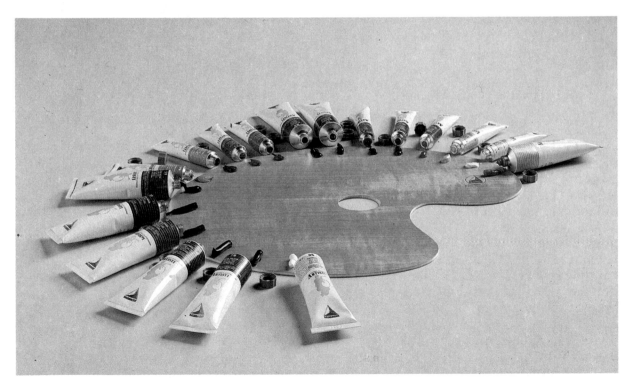

lean blue, turquoise, permanent green, emerald green, olive green, raw umber and zinc white. Always arrange your colours in this order, lining up the tubes before you squeeze out the paint. After a while, this arrangement will become automatic.

After years of practice with this palette, which is the one I use, you will start to add or subtract one paint or another to reflect your own taste. For example, I personally eliminated Veronese green, geranium lake, Prussian blue, the sepias, many of the browns, and violets and many of the reds, thereby reducing my palette to the essentials.

Manet's Lemon

It is often the small details that reveal a great painter. Let's look now at a painting of a lemon by Edouard Manet to analyse his composition, his handling of light and the colours he used.

First of all, notice the amount of yellow he used in comparison with the dark background. If you look at the reproduction with your eyes slightly closed, you will notice that the lemon occupies roughly one quarter of the paint surface; the other three-quarters are dark.

There is a rule of thumb that says the dark

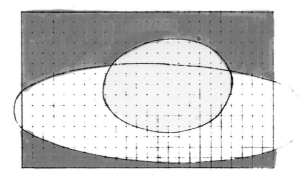

area of a canvas should be approximately three times that of the light area. This rule will help you to balance your compositions.

Returning to Manet's painting, we can see that the elements of the composition are very simple (another mark of a great painter is the ability to paint large canvases using very simple elements).

The lemon has an elliptical shape, as does the metal plate, which extends beyond the frame of the painting. There is about half as much space to the right of the lemon as there is to the left of the lemon. Similarly, the lemon has been positioned so that slightly more of it lies in the upper half of the painting. In fact there is more space below the lemon to the tabletop than there is above the lemon to the top edge of the painting.

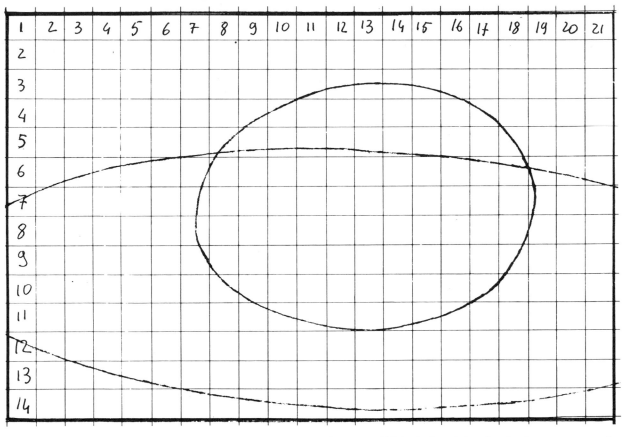

We should also note the dimensions of the composition. It is 14 cm (5½ in.) high and 21 cm (8¼ in.) wide; both fourteen and twenty-one are multiples of seven. If all this

Edouard Manet: 'The Lemon' (1880-1), 14 × 21cm. Musée d'Orsay, Paris.

seems complicated to you, keep in mind that these calculations are much simpler than the ones carried out in the past by Renaissance fresco painters and others. Today, such rules of construction tend to be ignored but it is worth remembering that in a painting not a colour, nor a line nor a curve is ever there purely by chance. Even Klee, Kandinsky, Malevich and others made such calculations.

But going back to our lemon, let's see if we can work out what colours Manet used so we can paint something similar.

Luisella Lissoni's Quince, Cup and Saucer

Using what we have just learned from Manet's composition, we can approach this next one with greater understanding.

Study the composition for a moment and then try to reconstruct the shape only, leaving the positioning of the fruit until later. Just as the plate and lemon in Manet's composition were elliptical in shape, so here the plate and the rim of the cup when seen in perspective, have similar shapes.

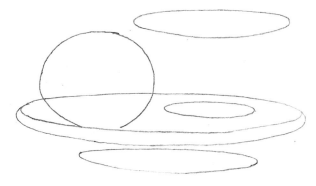

A white object tends to look larger than it actually is. In order to reduce the effect of this optical illusion, you may wish to neutralize the white. One way to do this is by placing it next to a colour. This reduces its volume without causing it to lose its luminosity. The quince, painted a warm yellow, serves this function particularly well. An orange or a persimmon would also be good choices.

It is a good idea to work on a dark background, in order to limit the number of light areas. Therefore I have placed the composition on an ochre-coloured ground with a light-coloured vertical zone and a darker nut-coloured zone.

You can try a similar composition yourself. Prepare your palette by arranging your colours as I described earlier. You will also need three stiff hair brushes, Nos 6, 8, and 12.

On a piece of wood 12 × 18 cm (4¾ × 7⅛ in.) prepared as I described on page 19, sketch your composition in pencil. Dilute the paint with white spirit, then take the largest brush and fill in the white areas with wide flat strokes to define the cup and plate, varying the tones by mixing white with bistre.

The area in the shadows should be a bluish bistre and the lighter area should be a yellowish bistre. Always begin with white and darken it by adding the bistre to it, rather than the other way around (unless you are starting with the shadows, in which case the procedure is exactly the opposite).

The yellow of the quince is cadmium yellow mixed with a little burnt sienna and white; for the darkest area, add a very small amount of bistre mixed with burnt umber.

The colour of the little ledge in the background is obtained by adding ultramarine to a mixture of Vandyke brown and white for the luminous part. For the vertical area, use the same colour with burnt sienna.

You can easily see the different brushstrokes. They tend to follow the lines of the object they are covering on the cup: for example, they are curved and, in the quince, they tend to be vertical; the horizontal surface is painted with horizontal strokes.

To reproduce a corner with two distinct areas, one in the light and the other in shadow, use a clean brush and work with a range of tones beginning with the shadows and moving gradually to the areas in the light. This way, your shading will be correct.

You can get some remarkable results using these techniques; they can also be used for special effects such as those ob-tained in Pellizza da Volpedo's still-life on the following page.

A Still-life by Pellizza da Volpedo
Pellizza da Volpedo, the youngest of the Italian Divisionists, was considered a minor artist by the critics of his day, mainly due to his political beliefs. His critics' understanding, however, was very superficial, and their prejudice has since been recognized by modern critics. The paintings of this great artist, whose work is comparable to Géricault, Daumier or Courbet, are again on display.

Let us turn to his still-life on the next page. He invented a new way of treating a common subject. After finishing this still-life, he took a dry, hair-type brush about 5 cm (2 in.) wide and dragged it over the still-wet paint, thereby creating a mass of colour that none-

Giuseppe Pellizza da Volpedo: 'Still-life with Grapes and Chestnuts' *(c. 1890), 48 × 77.5cm. Traversa Collection, Tortona.*

theless gives the impression of grapes.

The result has the air of something completely fortuitous. But it was not so. Pellizza himself wrote: *The internal process by which a painter produces one of his works for us can happen in one of two ways: either it comes from an idea that the artist conceived while looking for some suitable shape in nature to paint or it comes from a casual glance at something that then inspired him with an idea.*

This, and other works by Pellizza, anticipates by sixty years the so-called 'negation process' used by informal modern painters. As an analytical painter, he left nothing to chance. The smudges (obtained, as I said, by passing a dry brush over a finished painting) mix the colours and determine the look of the picture, which uses only four or five tones. I know of no other Italian painter of that period who went as far as he did. Obliterating the image in this way, with the painter destroying what he had so carefully constructed, was in itself a revolutionary act, and it forces a deep, dynamic, new emotion to be born. This new technique succeeds in expressing pain, something which can be perceived even in a simple still-life with grapes.

'Quinces' by Luisella Lissoni

Now let us examine a more classic composition. The objects in this painting have been arranged on the mantelpiece of a chimney. On each end, there is a piece of terracotta; on one end, a pot and on the other, a cup. In between, there are four quinces. The drawing was done in charcoal on an untreated hardboard support with its smooth side up.

The carefully studied use of colour reminds me of an Impressionist painting.

Look at the different tones in the background. There are bluish shadows under the mantelpiece and a lighter ochre colour below that, in the foreground. To compensate for the darker background behind the quinces, the artist has added less white to the ochre.

The quinces have been painted with ochre mixed with a little cadmium yellow and white. For the areas in shadow, the artist added ultramarine to the base colour while those areas that are in the light were obtained by adding zinc white.

A little burnt sienna has been mixed in for the warmest shadows.

The leaves were painted with ultramarine and cadmium yellow, a little Hooker's green and zinc white. To get darker, cooler colours, mix your green with ultramarine or indigo, depending on the colour you ultimately want to achieve.

For a warm shadow, going towards brown, add some carmine. The colour of the pot was obtained by mixing bistre with some burnt umber and a little white.

To suggest the roundness of the pot in the foreground, add some burnt sienna to the background colour. The luminous reflections were done with a clear grey that came from mixing white and bistre, while the lightest tones were obtained by adding the warm colour of the pot to white until a rosy tone was reached. Remember that to lighten a colour in your palette, you must start with white and add the darker colour and not the other way around.

The cup was rendered with a very light bistre to which was added a little ultramarine. The reflections are darker around the edges and yellowish in the parts closest to the fruit. The projected shadows (that is, those behind the objects) were obtained by adding different amounts of the background colour to a base of bistre, depending on the

Luisella Lissoni: 'Quinces' (1987), 62.6 × 20.7cm. The Artist's Collection.

56

intensity desired.

A characteristic feeling of movement has been given to the background through the use of criss-crossed brush-strokes.

Try to arrange some objects horizontally yourself, as in this composition. Before you begin to paint them, mix your colours carefully on your palette so you can achieve the same sort of effect. This effect can be found in many different styles of painting, including Expressionist art. The important thing is to learn to work correctly.

'Wisteria' by Gianni Maimeri

Gianni Maimeri lived during a period that was particularly difficult for Italian artists. It was dominated by the second wave of Futurists, who declared art dead. Maimeri himself managed to remain aloof from the polemics of his day. A sensitive artist, he was able to create some masterpieces, finding his inspiration in ordinary objects. From his many still-lifes, I have chosen this one of a delicate branch of wisteria, most likely painted with cobalt violet to which some cobalt blue and white have been added. The dark plate and background, even the very frame of the painting, remind me somewhat of Manet's 'The Lemon'. Today, still-life painting is not part of the curriculum for young painters, but it is worth remembering that the majority of the Cubists' paintings were inspired by still-lifes.

Gianni Maimeri: 'Wisteria' *(1930) 40 × 26 cm. Maimeri Family Collection.*

To discover the possibilities of expression that this genre of painting can inspire let us look next at a still-life by Cézanne.

'The Black Clock' by Paul Cézanne

Unlike van Gogh, Cézanne rarely discussed the subject of painting in his writings. But his work has been written about by many other famous people. One of them, Rainer Maria Rilke, wrote the following in a letter to his wife Clara Westhoff in 1907, a year after Cézanne's death.

Rue Cassette 29, Paris VIe 24 October 1907
'I said grey, yesterday, talking about the self-portrait's background of light bronze interlaced with grey motifs; what I should have said was a particular shade of metallic white, like aluminium, for, strictly speaking, grey is absent from Cézanne's works. To his eye, grey did not exist. He studied it closely and instead found violet or blue or russet or green. Above all, he found violet (a colour that had never before been used with such nuances and so meticulously) discovering it where we would find only grey and, on finding it, would rest content. More demanding than we, he, so to speak, unearthed hidden violets, the way certain evenings, especially in autumn, reveal them, drawing out the violet hidden in the greyness of the façades; and he did this so effectively that the colour can be found in all manner of tones from a vague and subtle lilac to the heavy purple of Finnish granite. Even though I said that, strictly speaking, there were no greys in his paintings (in his landscapes the presence or absence of ochre or burnt earth tones is too keenly felt to leave room for grey), Miss Vollmoeller pointed out that when one is surrounded by his landscapes, they exude a soft grey atmosphere. We agreed it was the balance of Cézanne's colours in which no single one predominates that accounts for this calm velvety atmosphere. Although it was one of his peculiarities to use colours like chrome yellow and burning red lake in their pure form for his lemons and apples, he knew how to confine their resonance within the canvas: this resonance is absorbed, as an ear absorbs sound, by the attendant blue, producing a muted response; in consequence one feels no sense of being accosted, whether from close at hand or from afar. His still-lifes are miraculously absorbed in themselves. First, there is the white cloth, so often used, which is strangely permeated

with a dominant local tone; then there are the things placed there, each of which shows and reveals itself completely. His use of white as a colour was completely natural: it and black formed the two extremes of his wide palette. In the lovely effect of a black stone mantelpiece with a clock, black and white (here, in the form of a cloth hanging down from the mantelpiece) behave as ordinary colours. On the white cloth there is a coffee cup with a dark-blue border, a fresh, ripe lemon, a cut-glass vase with a scalloped edge and on the far left a large strange-looking seashell with its shiny pink mouth-like opening facing us.

'The shell's red interior, lighter along the curves, is balanced by a stormy shade of blue in the wall which the gilt-framed mirror on the mantelpiece enlarges and deepens. In the mirror, we are struck with a new contrast: the milky rose of an opal vase on top of the black clock, which works as a double contrast (once by itself and once, a little softer, as its reflection). The object and its reflection in the mirror are clearly shown and almost musically differentiated by that double note; they are contained within the painting like a basket of fruit and leaves, and indeed, look as if they had been no more difficult to collect and display. I would like to go back to see the canvas once more. Unfortunately, it is no longer at the Salon; in a few days there will be a long stupid automobile exhibition with a single object: speed. I will say goodbye for today.'

Rilke's analysis of colour is very interesting. Certainly, the colour is the first thing that catches our eye in the painting. But the careful composition by the artist is also quite extraordinary.

Look, for example, at the white cloth. Its surface forms a rectangle, broken by vertical folds creating vertical lines rising towards the upper half of the painting. The fold of the napkin in the upper right corner forms an unequal triangle. The black clock reflected in the mirror forms a cube, while the moulding of the mirror frame and the crystal vase continue the vertical line of the folds of the cloth. The cup, the lemon and the ceramic object, along with the cloth form the horizontal line of the picture and the large oval shell contrasts with the cube of the clock.

It is very important to learn how to arrange the objects in a composition. I suggest you gather together objects of different shapes and practise arranging them into harmonious groupings as often as possible.

Paul Cézanne: 'The Black Clock' (1869-70), 54 × 73cm. Private Collection, Paris.

'A Basket of Fruit' by Michelangelo Merisi ('Caravaggio')

When I finally began to study painting, I spent several years practising still-life drawings. The first thing I learned was how to compose my subject, arranging the different shapes one against the other in order to form a single geometric figure that would encompass them all.

On the advice of my professors, I would often go to the Pinacoteca Ambrosiana in Milan to study Caravaggio's 'A Basket of Fruit'. Standing in front of that painting, I realised how little all the work I had done up till then amounted to. Quite simply, Caravaggio's painting is perfect. His use of space and the picture's construction are of an astonishing modernity.

The basket forms a truncated lozenge, at the base of which, on the right, lies another half-lozenge, formed by the branch and leaves of the vine in shadow. In the same way, the design of the wicker basket forms more lozenges. A series of half-lozenges or equilateral triangles start from the central lozenge.

The width of the brown line of the table top is one-third of the height of the basket; the upper edge of the basket is the same width as the horizontal half of the lozenges and also marks the horizon line of the composition. This means that to be seen correctly this painting must be hung in such a way that this line is at eye level.

The height of the basket plus the brown line represent exactly one-fifth of the total height of the painting. In addition, the light coming from above forms a 45 degree angle. If you look carefully and, with pencil and paper, calculate the lines of construction in this painting, you will discover that all manner of subtle geometry lies hidden in the composition.

Now let us turn to the colours. The colours used in Caravaggio's day are not the same as those in use today. For example, ultramarine blue was an extract of crushed lapis lazuli and at that time was very expensive. Incidentally, the raw material from which it came is virtually non-existent today. Now, the colour is produced chemically and its tone has clearly strayed somewhat from the old ultramarine. The background is composed of raw sienna and white. You can also use a titanium white. As you can see, the background is not a uniform colour, because an area lightened by sunlight can never be one solid colour. It offers many almost im-

Michelangelo Merisi ('Caravaggio'): 'A Basket of Fruit' (1595), *64 × 46 cm. Art Gallery, Ambrosiana, Milan.*

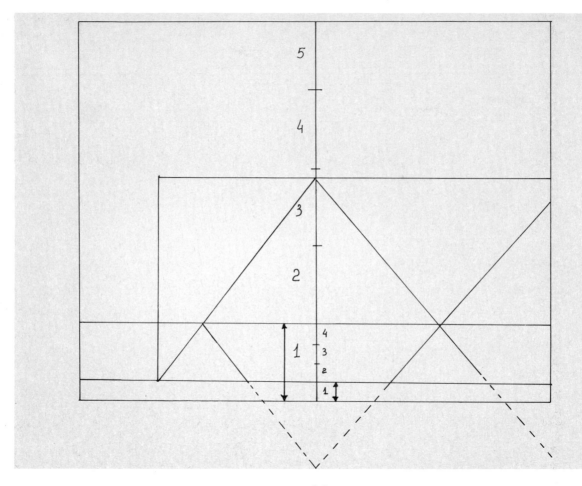

perceptible variations of tone and while they may all have the same intensity, some will be cooler or warmer than others. The basket is raw sienna with a little vermilion added to give it a warmer tone.

The greens are all mixed with a little red earth, such as burnt umber or burnt sienna.

As you can see, everything is very detailed except the vine leaves at the right, which are an almost uniform bluish-green, chosen precisely to give depth to the ensemble. Remember that to obtain this effect you must mix ultramarine blue with the colours.

Let us analyse the characteristics of the elements of the composition.

Unlike other painters of the period who used only perfect objects for their still-lifes, Caravaggio chose for his composition shrivelled and dried leaves half-eaten by insects, wormy apples, and grapes just beginning to rot. His choice of subject matter may well have reflected Caravaggio's feelings when he painted the picture.

Caravaggio was a painter of great talent and discipline. Like many others, he often worked in a genre of painting, such as the still-life, that was considered minor; nevertheless, he devoted as much attention to his still-lifes as to any of his larger paintings. In fact, he himself said, *'It is just as much work to paint a still-life with flowers as it is to paint one with figures.'*

Although as an artist he was disciplined, however, as a man his life was turbulent.

Michelangelo Merisi was born in Milan in 1571, but immediately after his birth his family moved to Caravaggio. In 1584 the painter was back in Milan, apprenticed to Simone Paterzano, a student of Titian. In 1592, however, he got into trouble with the law and fled Milan for Rome. There, in spite of the protection of the powerful cardinal Francesco Maria del Monte, he suffered a series of arrests and imprisonments. In 1600, he was accused of assault; in 1601, he was given a light sentence for wounding a soldier of the guard at the Castello San Angelo; in 1603, Giovanni Baglione sued him for slander. More arrests followed in 1604: one for throwing a plate of artichokes at a waiter and another for throwing stones at some guards. In November he was sent to prison for insulting an officer. The year 1605 was no better. In May, Caravaggio was arrested for carrying illegal weapons; on 20th July he was imprisoned for having offended a woman and her daughter. On the 29th of the same month, he was arrested for assaulting a notary after an argument over a woman named Lena, 'wife of Michelangelo'.

The most serious episode took place the following year. On 28th May, 1606 Caravaggio killed a certain Ranuccio Tommasoni over a wager on a tennis game and in an attempt to avoid a very heavy sentence, he fled Rome and hid in Naples. By 1607 he was in Malta and the following year he was named a knight of the Maltese Order. But his troubles were not over. On 6th October two men were on his trail after yet another escape, this time from prison where he had been locked up because of a quarrel with an officer of the law. Once more back in Italy, Caravaggio died in Porto Ercole at the early age of thirty-nine. He was struck down by fever.

An Exercise with an Apple
In memory of Caravaggio and his painting,

we will look at how to paint a realistic-looking apple.

The first thing you must do is start with a very good drawing that clearly defines the light and shadows. Divide the apple in two halves, one in the light and the other in shadow. The shadowy half, painted with a flat tint, should be rendered with a mixture of ultramarine blue and burnt umber diluted with white spirit.

Let it dry for twenty-four hours, then with very diluted colour go back over your painting again, adding accented layers of bluish-white to the shaded parts and a little dirty white, made by adding cadmium yellow to white, to the highlighted zones.

This technique is called scumbling or glazing and it consists of applying a very diluted layer of transparent colour over the base coat. This second colour may be lighter or darker, warmer or cooler than the colour it covers.

Put the details in last, using a very fine sable-hair brush with a rounded point, and colour that has been diluted with turpentine.

Edouard Manet: 'Pinks and Clematis'
(1882), 56 × 35cm. Musée d'Orsay, Paris.

'Pinks and Clematis' by Edouard Manet

Edouard Manet (1832-1883), after receiving his formal training from Couture, a teacher at the École des Beaux-Arts, worked with Courbet from 1855 onwards. There he learned to construct works with large masses of colour and contrasts of light. This emphasis on colour and light resulted in his rejection by the Salon (the art establishment's annual exhibition of paintings which were chosen by the teaching staff of the École des Beaux-Arts) in 1859. He was rejected again in 1863, as event described by John Rewald in *A History of Impressionism*.

'In 1863 the jury was even more severe than it had been in previous years, owing, it appears, to the uncompromising attitude of M. Signol, Renoir's teacher at the École des Beaux-Arts; neither Ingres nor Delacroix participated in the deliberations. This time many artists who had been more or less regularly admitted before, like Manet, were turned down. According to one of his friends, Manet had called on Delacroix to ask for his support before the jury, but the old master was too ill to attend the sessions. He managed, however, to visit the exhibition at Martinet's where Manet showed fourteen canvases, among them "Lola de Valence", "Spanish Dancers", and "Concert in the Tuileries Gardens". Aroused by visitors laughing in front of these works or threatening to tear them up, Delacroix, upon leaving, said loudly: "I regret not to have been able to defend this man."

'The deliberations of the jury started on April 2, and three days later rumours had already begun to circulate that its members were committing a veritable "massacre". When, on April 12, the official results were announced, it turned out that of some five thousand paintings submitted by about three thousand artists (many sending in only a single work), the jury had rejected three-fifths. Nobody could remember a similar proportion of refusals.'

In 1882, a year before his death, Manet painted this very simple vase of flowers.

For this work, Manet started with the background, and it is very likely that he did not use any black at all, beginning instead with a mixture of the three primary colours, red, yellow and blue, or a mixture of emerald green and carmine. As you can see, the background is not a uniform colour. In the lower half, it catches the reflection of the lighter-coloured base, a blend of yellow ochre with zinc white. A little of the background colour mixed with some bistre gives us the shade he used for the leaves. You will notice that the upper leaves are darker than the lower ones.

If you look carefully, you can see that to the right of the pinks, the background is bluer. This blue patch makes the background vibrate and it also fills up the empty space, which would be more noticeable if it were all one colour. It is also a good contrast to the purple of the clematis. All of the greens he used were a mixture of a little cadmium yellow and ultramarine blue. Whether you mix lighter or darker greens, or cooler or warmer ones, you should always work with the same tone. Manet based his pinks on vermilion to which he added a little carmine and white.

It is always difficult for a beginner to paint a transparent object, such as a glass vase. Here is how to begin. Look at the vase carefully for a few minutes, then put down on the canvas the colours you see. You may have to practise a few times, but eventually you will begin to get good results.

I have attempted to explain something of what Manet's method might have been as he painted this canvas. Clearly, every painter has his own methods, but you can practise by taking the same kinds of flowers Manet used and a vase or glass identical to the one in the painting; then use my description of Manet's colours and try to re-create this painting yourself.

Even though Manet's talent was recognized by many famous figures, he spent the greater part of his life battling the incomprehension of critics and art dealers. The following extract is taken from *The Art Dealer* by Christian Herchenröder and explains what has happened since then to Manet's works.

'. . . *As for Manet, the possibilities for profiting from the prices being fetched on the market for exceptional works are very limited. According to Reitlinger, the only important work of his to come on the market in the 1960s was a painting from 1866, "The Smoker" (100 × 80 cm). It was sold at auction in New York in 1965 for only $450,000 and then displayed the following year at the Tribune Gallery. This may be a harsh judgement but it is a fair one; it was confirmed again in the 70s. In 1973, the Wildenstein Gallery valued a still-life with fish, an average work, at $1,400,000.*

'*The Impressionist collection of Antonio Santamarina in Buenos Aires, broken up in*

1974 after a sale at Sotheby's, did not sell for very impressive prices, partly because the sale seems to have come to the attention of the heirs, who put pressure on the Argentine authorities to raise an official protest before the auction even began, and also because the sale took place at a unfavourable time, early autumn 1973, right in the middle of a depression in the market for Impressionist paintings. Even though it was an important sale and well-attended, among the unsold paintings was one from 1860, "The Students from Salamanca". It is not known whether an unfinished painting, "Isabelle Lemonnier with Muff", a work estimated to be worth £200,000 or £300,000, suffered the same fate; the fact remains that the hammer fell at £100,000, bid.'

'Woman with Chrysanthemums' by Edgar Degas

'Up to now, he is the man who has known better than anyone else how to capture the spirit of modern life.' This is how Edmond de Goncourt defined Edgar Degas in 1874.

The early life of this painter was in the classic mould. He alternated between lessons with Ingres and the study of the great masters in museums, especially the Louvre.

In fact, it was there that he met Manet. The two artists had much in common. They both had reserved, refined characters, and came from solid bourgeois families. A strong friendship grew up between them, although Manet often criticized his friend for some of his choices of historical subjects. But Degas, who was influenced by Manet even for his historical paintings, used real people for models; he rejected Ingres's rules about choosing a subject first then having a model strike a pose to suit the subject. He said that he wanted to capture people going about their daily lives and, above all, to give faces the same degree of expression usually reserved for the body. As you can see in the drawing reproduced on the next page, Degas studied natural poses in detail and in his works he made pose the most important element of a composition.

To understand Degas better, let us read what he wrote in his journal:

'What is certain is that to arrange something from nature and to draw it are two very different things.

'There are good people badly turned out; there are, I think, even more bad ones well turned out.

'One does not like to hear someone say, as

71

Edgar Degas: Study for Dame Hertel
('Woman with Chrysanthemums')
(1865), 37.5 × 23.3cm. Pencil.
Fogg Art Museum, Cambridge,
Massachusetts

Edgar Degas: 'Woman with
Chrysanthemums' *(1865),*
71 × 92cm. Oil on canvas.
Metropolitan Museum of Art,
New York.

if to a child, when speaking of rosy cheeks and shining complexions, "Ah, what life, what blood." Human skin is as varied in its appearance, especially among us, as the rest of nature – fields, trees, mountains, lakes, forests. There is about as much chance of finding a resemblance between a person and a pebble as there is between two pebbles; in fact, everyone knows that one is more likely to see two people who resemble each other somewhat (I am speaking of colouring, the question of shape is something else – one can often find a resemblance between a stone and a fish, a mountain and the head of a dog, clouds and horses, etc.).

'So, it is not only instinct that says one must look at the colours of everything in order to see the affinities between the things that are alive, the things that are dead, and the things that are vegetating. I can easily remember the colour of certain hair, for example, because it struck me that it looked like varnished walnut or oakum or the bark from an horse chestnut, real hair with its suppleness and lightness or its hardness and heaviness. And one paints in so many different ways, on so many kinds of supports that a tone will be one colour here and another there. Not to mention the contrasts which distort things even more.

'In Paris, it is possible to live next door to a man who wants to paint Turks, while you want to paint Arabs and, for that reason alone, you find yourselves the masters of two contrasting points of view.

'The paintings of Moreau are the dilettantism of a great-hearted man if one thinks only of the subject, and of a noble-minded man if one looks only at what he has done.

'Make of the expressive head (the Academy style) a study of modern sentiments – that comes from Lavater, but somehow a more relative Lavater. Study the observations of Delsarte on the expressive movements of the eye. Its beauty must be in only a certain physiognomy.

'Work hard on the effects of evening, lamps, candles, etc. The interesting part is not always to show the source of light, but its effect.

'Not to see it – is it possible?

'Draw a lot. Ah, the good drawing . . .

'Think of a treatise on adornments for women or by women, of the way they observe and combine things, the way they get dressed. Much more than men, they compare a thousand things to each other every day.

'If I rise early, I can still redeem my very dissolute existence...

'Paint and draw people in familiar and typical poses, and above all give their faces the same range of expression that one gives their bodies. That is, if someone laughs a lot, show them laughing. Of course there are certain feelings that one cannot depict for the sake of decency, as some portraits are not only for us, the painters. What a lot of subtle nuances to put in!'

Notebooks 22 and 23

Now, let us take a look at the composition of Degas's painting 'Woman with Chrysanthemums', which was completed in 1865. This will help us when we come to the next chapter and study the figure.

Clearly, the flowers in the centre are the focal point of the painting, while the glass pitcher on the left works as a balance for the figure on the right.

The mass of flowers fits within an imaginary triangle, as does the area comprising the vase, the pitcher and the space between them. The two triangles together form a square while the female figure occupies a rectangular space whose surface takes up about one-third of the canvas.

The colours have been dabbed on with vertical strokes vaguely recalling pencil marks, and Degas's palette is identical to Manet's.

It is also interesting to look at Degas's preparatory study in pencil. Before painting a picture, it is a good idea to get into the habit of drawing it first. The drawing will then serve as a pattern for your painting. Draw on a sheet of cartridge paper the same size as the final painting. Begin by laying down a system of grids on both the drawing and the canvas. Then when you have finished your drawing, you can transfer it to the canvas using the lines in your grid as reference points.

Another technique for transferring a drawing to your canvas is 'pouncing'. In this method you first use a needle to prick holes in your drawing, to outline it, and then you attach the drawing to your canvas with adhesive tape.

Next, you place the canvas on a flat surface, and lightly rub charcoal or umber-coloured powder (sold in muslin bags in artists' suppliers) over it with a piece of fine cloth so that it penetrates the holes. Finally, spray the canvas with fixative so that the tiny marks do not disappear when you begin.

THE FIGURE

I have described how to draw the figure in other handbooks. The general rules are always the same and we will look at some of them in this, and the following, chapter. The important thing is constantly to practise drawing different parts of the human body, copying details from anatomy books if you cannot find life-drawing classes.

Every painter has spent a great deal of time studying the body, even abstract painters like Picasso, Mondrian and Klee – as you can see from the drawings below. These are proof that, contrary to what certain experts in the last fifty years have suggested, abstract painters *have* studied the human figure.

The art market is a world of its own. Let us find out some more about it from Christian Herchenröder whom we met in the last chapter.

Paul Klee: Anatomy Study *(1902). Black pencil. Klee Foundation, Berne.*

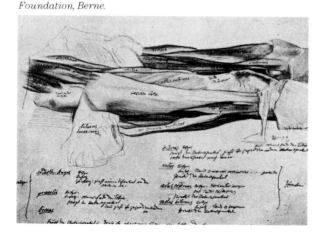

The Art Market, a Faithful Reflection of the Modern Economy

'An art dealer, now no longer living, asked me in 1975 how it was that I had decided to specialize in a market that only interested a few business men and amateurs. The answer is simple: this market with its great demands and its enormous contorting of the spirit, is a perfect reflection of the vicissitudes of the economy today. It is a consumer's market yet it still has great resources; it is a commercial branch of business that attracts investment according to the state of the economic cycle.

'If you look at prices, you will discover manipulation as well as artificial trend-setting, you will find over-priced objects and completely neglected areas, and you will find speculators, crooks and adventurers who too often will make you doubt the seriousness of the market.

'Like it or not, we must be aware that in an era of open economies, art becomes a capital investment as a vehicle for short-term speculation and a means of escaping the taxmen. The more inflation increases, the greater demand there is for art, and this is in perfect agreement with the persuasive Anglo-Saxon slogan, "Art is the best hedge against inflation." The art consumer, a character of whom we will say more further on, is a consumer in the strictest sense of the word. That is, he is someone who profits from the possibilities offered by free exchange to carry out business deals, whether good or bad, just like anyone else carrying out any other deal. He who sees this market as honest as any other, simply regulated by supply and demand, remains outside the game.'

As we have seen, the art market does not have much to do with the inspiration of painters!

Even great artists in the past, working for princes, accepted their commissions and then modified them to suit their own interests. It is for this reason that when frescos are restored one often finds different paintings from the final composition revealed underneath the top layers of paint.

The revolt against the establishment in Italy came with the Italian Impressionists. Many of them participated in the Italian *Risorgimento*; among them were many· anarchists, hunted and persecuted by the Austrian police. Caffi, for example, died in combat. Zandomeneghi fled to France. Polit-

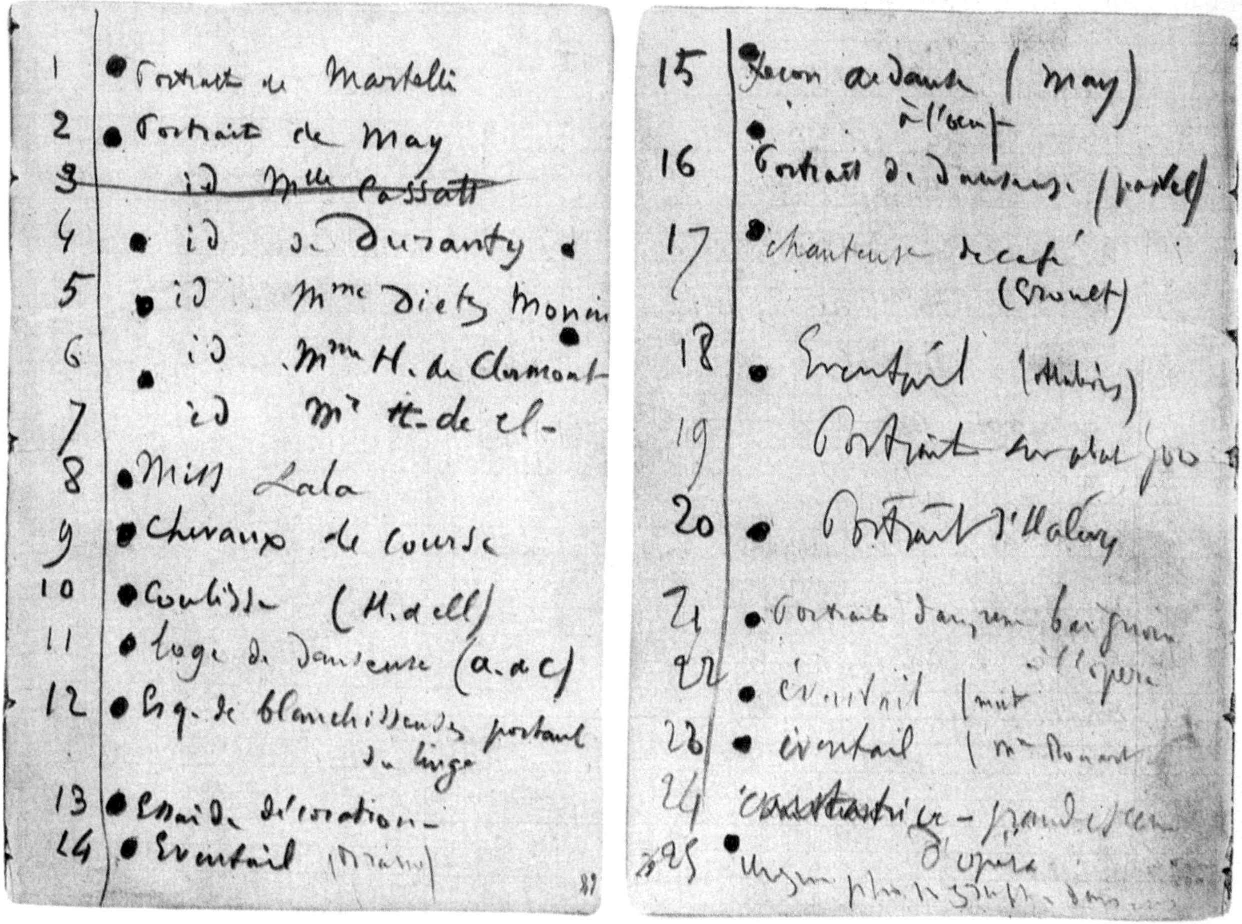

1 • Portrait de Martelli
2 • Portrait de May
3 ~~id Mlle Cassatt~~
4 • id de Duranty
5 • id Mme Dietz Monnin
6 • id Mme H. de Clermont
7 id Mr H. de Cl.
8 • Miss Lala
9 • Chevaux de course
10 • Coulisse (M. d'Ell)
11 • Loge de danseuse (a. a c)
12 • Grp. de blanchisseuses portant du linge
13 • Essai de décoration
14 • Eventail (Diano)

15 Leçon de danse (May) à l'œuf
16 • Portrait de danseuse (pastel)
17 • Chanteuse de café (Sronet)
18 • Eventail (Melbis)
19 Portrait au plus joue
20 • Portrait d'Halévy
21 • Portrait d'une bourguonne à l'Opéra
22 • Eventail (nut)
23 • Eventail (Mme Monet)
24 Caricature - grand dessin d'Opéra
25 • Un nymphe ...... danseuse

List of works by Degas for the fourth Impressionist exhibition (1879). Martelli's name is first on the list.

ical motifs and pictorial motifs brought the two movements together. One Italian, a critic who came into contact with artists from both countries, exhibited a group of Italian paintings in France and a group of French paintings in Italy. This critic was Diego Martelli and his artist friends often used him as a subject for their paintings.

De Nittis set himself up in Paris and his house attracted some of the best-known personalities in France. In his salon Manet, Degas, Zola and others often met. Through him, Martelli joined the group and there he met Pissarro who gave him two paintings (which hang today in the Modern Art Gallery in Florence). It was during this period that Degas painted Martelli's portrait. There are two versions of it, with preliminary sketches for each. After Paris, Martelli began to write articles for Italian journals and in 1879, when he returned to Italy, he gave a memorable lecture which included the first account of the work of the Impressionist painters.

'Diego Martelli' by Edgar Degas
Degas made several sketches for the portrait, the most curious of which is the one reproduced here from one of his notebooks. It is a quick sketch, achieved with only a few

79   *Edgar Degas:* Study for the portrait of Diego Martelli.

Edgar Degas: 'Portrait of Diego Martelli' *(1879), 110 × 100cm. Oil on canvas. National Gallery of Scotland, Edinburgh.*

lines. Note the creases in the jacket on the left arm. With only a few short strokes, he has managed to express the image of an arm in movement. Similarly, although the beard and hair are only lightly sketched, they suggest fullness and volume.

Degas chose an almost square canvas and on it drew a very free composition; each object seems to be there by chance. The figure of Martelli and the table next to him form vertical lines that are balanced by the horizontal lines of the painting and the sofa in the background.

The figure itself is painted with broad strokes, characteristic of Degas's pastels. The painting is made up of a juxtaposition of colours with few details filled in – look at the newspaper in the upper right of the table. The printing is completely indistinguishable.

The light falls in two areas, one, in the left foreground, less defined than the other. That is made up of a slightly darker vertical area along the edge of the painting with a lighter triangular patch below it. The light also falls on the newspaper in the right middle ground which, compared with the other two areas, is somewhat bluer.

The centre of the newspaper (the part in deepest shadow) is rendered with a combi-nation of bistre and white. The part of the newspaper just under the fold, in full light, was obtained with a lighter shade of bistre.

Nuances are obtained by mixing base colours with warmer or cooler colours according to where they will be placed. Great painters often use such juxtapositions of colour, constantly comparing the subject and the painting, and mentally trying to superimpose one over the other, like a pair of slides.

'Diego Martelli in Castiglioncello' by Giovanni Fattori

In the middle of the nineteenth century, while France was going through great social change, Italy was struggling to win its independence. Many Italian artists fought in the wars for independence and lost their lives.

During this period, a group of artists in Florence gathered in the Café Michelangelo. According to Telemaco Signorini, they had been part of the Lombardy Campaign in 1848 and participated in the defence of Venice, Bologna and Rome in 1849. The patron and guardian angel of these painters, who were dubbed '*Macchiaioli*', was Diego Martelli. He helped them financially to the point of nearly squandering his fortune and he championed them against their critics.

During the summer of 1858 Degas and Gustave Moreau also went often to this café (a modern bar with the same name still exists in Via Cavour). Degas, in particular, became friendly with some of the Florentine painters, one of whom was Giovanni Fattori.

Fattori painted this oil on wood around 1867. He often used wood as a support, but what is more curious is that he often took his wood from cigar boxes and used it as it was, with no further preparation.

The colour has been painted on lightly and as a result the wood can be seen underneath, giving the painting the effect of one tone upon another. The work is quite small, only 13 × 20 cm (5⅛ × 7⅞ in.) and is made up of small spots of colour. In fact the name 'Macchiaioli' comes from the Italian word for 'spot', after the technique of brushing on spots or dabs of paint which characterized the works of this group of painters. The name 'Macchiaioli' was derisively given to them by a critic, just as the term 'Impressionist' was originally pejorative.

The 'spot', as Telemaco Signorini said, 'was, at the beginning, meant to heighten "chiaroscuro", or light and shadow, and the use of this technique became a way for these painters to distinguish themselves from the old masters. The "Macchiaioli" sacrificed mass and relief in their paintings for the heightened clarity of their figures.' The colours they chose were not 'invented' as they were in studio paintings, but 'seen'.

Let me explain what I mean. A painter looks at his subject attentively, with half-closed eyes, precisely so that he can analyse what he sees and then transfer it to his canvas. But, before you apply your colour to the support, you should work it out first on the palette. Then try it out with the other colours on the canvas by dabbing a small amount in the area where you want it. If the colour seems to be balanced, fine. If, it is not quite right, add a little white or one of the other warmer or cooler tones on your palette, as necessary. Look, for example, at the red hat and the red cart in the background on the upper right-hand side of Fattori's painting. Originally, these two colours were one and the same, vermilion. But as the hat is in shadow, the artist has added a little burnt umber to the vermilion, while the cart sitting in the sunlight was painted with vermilion mixed with yellow ochre and a little white.

When my students are starting out, they often ask me the best way to begin a painting. I will teach you an old method used in

Giovanni Fattori: 'Diego Martelli in Castiglioncello' *(c. 1867), 13 × 20cm. Oil on wood. Private Collection, Milan.*

painting frescos, called underpainting or 'sinopia'. Prepare some bistre (made, as I explained earlier), and dilute it heavily. Then add zinc white until you get a colour that is exactly the same as asphalt. Apply this wash to the areas of your canvas that will be in shadow, both for the figures and for the landscape, using it to draw and shade them. This will give you a monochromatic base for all the volumes in the painting. After that, all you have to do is fill in the colours. Start either with the foreground or with the most important figure, then continue on to the subjects in the middle ground. It will be easier to find the intermediate colours if you work in this way. Underpainting also enables you to produce the remarkable illusion of depth that great painters so often achieve.

Returning now to Fattori, we can imagine that he worked as follows. Starting with the shirt, he got its colour by mixing raw umber with a little cerulean and a little white, heavily diluting it with turpentine. By adding some raw umber to this mixture and diluting that with turpentine as well, he got the colour for the trees, which, as you can see, comes from the same colour range as the shirt. The ground in the shadows is also based on the colour of the shirt, with just a

little more white added. And, to give his tones more variety, Fattori also took advantage of the dark nut colour of his wooden support.

For the sky and the sea, he probably used ultramarine blue and white, adding a little cerulean and a great deal of white to them for the sky. The best way to mix light colours is to prepare a small amount of colour on a corner of your palette. Then rinse your brush with turpentine and dry it by brushing it over a piece of chiffon. Next, take some white and add the colour to the white until you have the desired shade. If you work the other way around, starting out with a colour and adding white to it, you will find that you have a lot more colour than you need.

After finishing the sky and the sea, Fattori worked on the middle ground. With yellow ochre, white and a little cadmium yellow, he painted the ground in the shadowy light behind the trees and the dappled ground around the figure where the light filters through the leaves. By mixing a little of the colour of the ground in shadow with a dot of the yellow ochre of the ground in the sun, he obtained the colour of Martelli's chair. His shoes are the same colour as the trees, and so are the trousers, but with perhaps a little more emerald green added. He got the colour for the grassy area close to the sea by mixing permanent green, a little Veronese green and white, and then by adding small amounts of burnt sienna and emerald green, he was able to make all the other shades of green. The flesh tones come from mixing raw sienna, a little vermilion and white. For the shadows, he has added burnt umber for the cool shades and burnt sienna for the warm.

The colour for the shirt worn by the man sitting next to the cart was obtained by mixing the colour used for the ground with a little of that used for the sky. The artist used the same colour with which he painted the trees for the shadowy areas of the house. The roofs were painted with burnt sienna mixed with a little white, while the façade of the smallest house, in full sunlight, is white, muddied with a little yellow ochre, as is the little road that leads away from the large house on the left. Its sunlit façade was obtained by mixing the light colour of the ground with the colour used for the trees.

You will have noticed in this description how one colour is used as a base for a neighbouring colour and how these two colours then give you a third. You should try to work in this way.

'Diego Martelli' by Federico Zandomeneghi

The many portraits of Diego Martelli are testimony to his popularity with painters. This one was painted by Federico Zandomeneghi.

Zandomeneghi, born in Venice in June 1841, came from a family of artists – both his father and grandfather were well-known sculptors and friends of Antonio Canova. Together, they created a monument to Titian that today is in the Frari Church in Venice.

At the age of fifteen, Zandomeneghi began studying at the Fine Arts Academy in Venice. Three years later, he left his birthplace to escape obligatory military service in the Austro-Hungarian army and moved to Pavia. In 1860, he joined the 'Expedition of the Thousand' with Garibaldi. He went back to Venice in 1862 to see his family but was arrested and sent to prison in Rovigo. Thanks to his father's intervention, he was released and went to Florence. There he met the artists who gathered at the Café Michelangelo and became part of the 'Macchiaioli' movement. The years from 1862 to 1866 were crucial in his development as an artist. He moved on to Paris in 1874.

In Paris, Zandomeneghi discovered the

Federico Zandomeneghi: 'Portrait of Diego Martelli' *(1879), 72 × 92cm. Oil on canvas. Modern Art Gallery, Pitti Palace, Florence.*

Impressionists and set himself up at 7 Rue Tourlaque where Toulouse-Lautrec and Suzanne Valadon (Utrillo's mother) lived. He remained there until his death in 1917.

This portrait of Martelli dates from the period when he was living in Paris. The composition is lively and dynamic, with a dimension that might almost be called cinematic.

Remember what we said about the colours in Fattori's painting of Martelli, and then look at the way Zandomeneghi achieved his effects. The background colour is essentially the sum of the colours used for the trousers and the jacket; the red of the armchair comes from the colour of the cup on the mantelpiece and the dark bistre of the console is repeated in the chair in the background, in the floor on the right and in the beard. This use of colour gives balance and harmony to the composition as a whole.

The Rules of Construction

In order to paint a figure correctly, you should know something at least of the rules of construction. The modern rules are those laid down by Schmidt in 1849 and perfected by Fritsch in 1895; they are called Fritsch's rules. These rules apply to the frontal view of a standing human figure, and are based on a

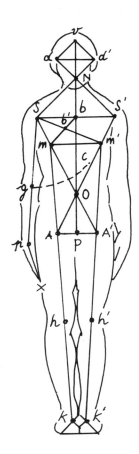

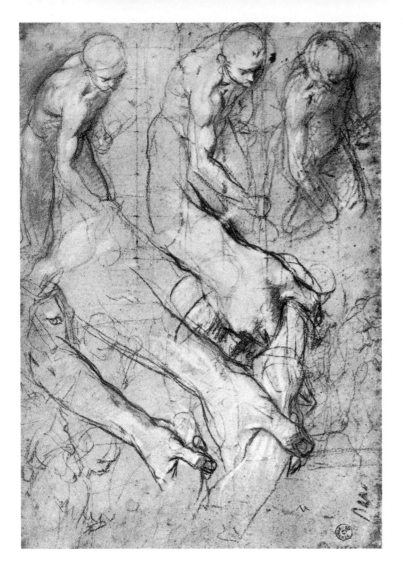

Federico Fiori 'Barocci': Studies for St Joseph, 42 × 283cm. Black stone with white highlights on blue paper. Offices, Florence.

Paul Cézanne: Amorous Couple, Outdoors (1859-75), 17.5 × 23.1cm. Pencil. Collection of Cézanne's Children, Paris.

straight line drawn downwards from the tip of the nose (N) to the groin (P).

The line NP is then divided into four equal parts, N-b, b-c, c-o and o-P. If above point N one adds another segment the same length as each of the preceding segments, one gets the dimension of the head. Using the same measure to the right and left of point b, you get points S and S' which define the width of the shoulders.

Starting from points S and S', draw two diagonal crossed lines that pass through point N and you will get points d and d' which correspond to the width of the head.

Using point P as the centre, draw a line parallel to line s-s' the same width as the head and you have the position of the joints of the legs at points A and A'. By joining points AS' and A'S, you get two lines that cross at point O, corresponding to the navel.

If from point b you trace a line parallel to line S-d', you get point m; from there, by tracing from point m a line parallel to line s-s', you will have point m'. These two points, m-m', correspond to the chest.

The length of line S-m' is the same as the length of the upper arm (s-g), while the distance between the chest and the navel gives you the line m-O, which is the same as the length of the forearm (g-p). The distance between the navel and the leg joint (O-A) corresponds to the length of the hand (p-x).

A-h, corresponding to the length of the thigh, is equal to m-A and the length of the knee and calf (h-k) is equal to m-A'. The height of the foot is equal to one-quarter of the measure of the head.

Painters have always studied the figure systematically. Look at these two pages, one taken from the sketchbook of Federico Fiori (called 'Barocci'), and the other from Cézanne's notebook. Barocci followed the classic method of measuring, which stated that the human body can be drawn using the head as the basic unit of measure.

Now look at the page from Cézanne's notes. He undoubtedly took more liberties with the rules but nevertheless his figures are no less well proportioned.

'French Soldiers, 1859' by Giovanni Fattori

In 1859, Italy was at war. There were scenes of battle everywhere: dead soldiers and horses, soldiers with haggard eyes walking through desolate fields; poor people leading a miserable existence. Artists' countrymen were at arms, like the soldiers in this marvellous work by Fattori.

This is one of Fattori's first paintings using *Macchiaioli* techniques. The subject was taken from real life, and reveals an extraordinary sense of colour that can be compared to Telemaco Signorini's experiments somewhat earlier. The colour is spread over the canvas to create a rigorous play of empty and filled-in spaces, with the light and shadows arranged to give the fugitive impression of a coloured chessboard. The separation of light and shadow is clean and clear, reduced to essentials, and with no intermediate tones. Each soldier's backpack is a different colour. The colour of the wall, like that of the background, is a mixture of umber and ceru-

Giovanni Fattori: 'French Soldiers, 1859' (1859), 15.5 × 32cm. Oil on canvas. Private Collection, Milan.

lean. You might try to reproduce these colours yourself by preparing them on your palette and then applying them to a small piece of black plywood. A cigar box would be even better, since then you would be working with the same support as Fattori.

To give you a glimpse of the character of the 'Macchiaioli' artists, look at the drawing by Telemaco Signorini on the left. It reads:

'A Baptism
'Watch' and he spat and gently
    spread the spit over the black wood.
'Look' and he spat again. 'Look at that
    little face – it's the baby Jesus...!'
'Could be. I don't know anything about
    such things.'
'It looks like a Carlino Dolci.'
'No, wait, it's not a Carlino. Anyway, it's
    painted on pear wood.'
And he spat again. 'It's a Perugino...!'
'Well, how did he get that figure
    wrapped up in a cloak...?'
'It's St Joseph. Can't you see?
Listen, it's surely by a great master
    and it's really a beauty.'
'Wait,' and he spat one last time.
'Do you want to know who it's by?
It's a Raphael...!'

92

Some Remarks on the Soldiers

If you would like to try an exercise like Fattori's, get out your box of paints, your pencils, a small piece of wood as a support and some turpentine and look for a place to paint where you can observe soldiers unnoticed.

For my drawing I found some policemen who had stopped a car; then I got as close to them as I could without being seen and I drew the little sketch in figure 1.

Once you have found a subject, fill in the shadows with a soft pencil or piece of charcoal. Then go over the shadows you have done in pencil with a little round-tipped hair-type brush dipped in turpentine. You will find that the turpentine dilutes the graphite of the pencil or the charcoal and gives your drawing an even grey tone.

Next make up some bistre and go over all the shaded areas of the uniform which you have smudged with your pencil. Prepare the flesh tones for the face and hands with yellow ochre, white and vermilion. For the parts of the face in shadow, add a little bistre to the flesh tones. With bistre and white, define the light areas of the uniform and the shoes. Use red for the stripe in the trousers, and add a little carmine to it for the part in shadow.

'Before the Print-Seller's' by Honoré Daumier

In a society that pollutes rivers and the air, destroying plants and animals, it is the big cities that determine whether or not you are a good painter. And how do they define a good painter? Unfortunately, it seems to be he who plays the game, that is, the artist who responds to the demands of the marketplace, often to the detriment of his art.

Impressionism was one movement that chose its own direction; it was not one whose direction was chosen for it.

The spirit of Impressionism breathes in this poem by Baudelaire, and calls to mind Cézanne, van Gogh and Pissarro.

ABEL AND CAIN

Race of Abel, sleep and feed,
God is pleased;

grovel in the dirt and die,
Race of Cain.

Race of Abel, your sacrifice
flatters the nostrils of the Seraphim;

Race of Cain, is your punishment
never to know an end?

Race of Abel, your fields prosper,
your cattle grow fat;

Race of Cain, your belly clamours
like a famished dog.

Race of Abel, warm yourself
at the hearth of your fathers;

shiver in the jackal's den,
Race of Cain.

Race of Abel, increase and multiply,
even your gold will breed;

though your heart burn, Race of Cain,
beware great appetites.

Race of Abel, build your cities
even as the ants;

Race of Cain, your children beg
for bread beside the road.

Race of Abel, your corpse
will fatten the reeking earth;

your labour, Race of Cain,
is not yet done.

Race of Abel, behold your shame:
the sword yields to the butcher-knife!

Rise up, Race of Cain,
and cast God down upon the earth!

Charles Baudelaire

Baudelaire's poetry might well have been written in honour of Daumier.

In spite of the difficulties they encountered when they were working to establish themselves, Ingres, Corot and Delacroix were both fortunate in their careers and also came from fairly comfortable backgrounds. Daumier, on the other hand, came from a very poor family.

He was born in Marseilles in 1808 and brought up in Paris. He began his artistic career drawing political cartoons for a satirical journal. These drawings became famous but along with fame, they also brought him swift condemnation and arrest.

Meanwhile, he had taken up painting. He served his informal apprenticeship at the Louvre, copying the statues of the great masters, and this early training gave his paintings a unique and characteristic look. Daumier worked especially hard on line and contour to create the volume that others achieved in their paintings through the use of colour alone. His colour range is sombre but intense, and it reflects an even, rhythmic use of light and shadow that comes from his aversion to dissonant colours.

Towards 1860, Daumier started to become known for his paintings as well as his illustrations. Sometimes considered a modern Don Quixote (Cervantes's idealistic and strange, yet genial, hero), in part because he illustrated Don Quixote's adventures, Daumier also revealed the goodness of his own soul by helping less fortunate artists.

Unfortunately his paintings did not bring him wealth. Daumier was forced to return to work for the newspaper for which he had produced his lithographs. By 1873, he was almost penniless and, to make matters worse, he was going blind. He was unable to pay his rent and his landlord threatened him

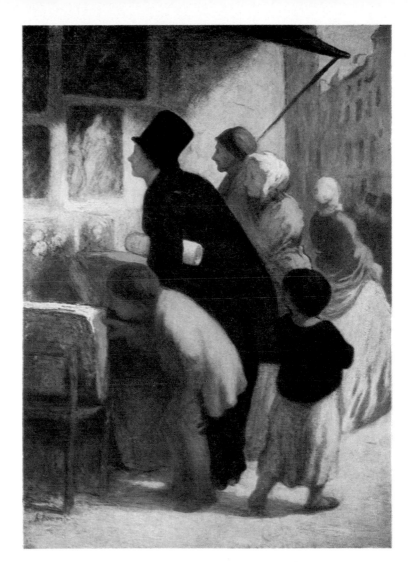

*Honoré Daumier: 'Before the Print-Seller's'
(c. 1860-5), 33 × 25cm. Oil on canvas.
Private Collection.*

with eviction. At this point, other more fortunate artists came to the rescue. Corot, in particular, wrote to him: *'My dear friend, I own a house in Valmondois, very close to Isel-Adam which is empty and it seems to me the best thing to do is to give it to you. I have had a contract drawn up by my notary. I am not doing it for you but simply to annoy your landlord!*

With all my affection, yours, Corot.'

Daumier retired to Valmondois and died in that house in 1879, completely blind. A few years later, some art dealers bought the works he had left behind from his widow for ridiculous prices.

Daumier did not date his paintings and this makes it difficult to know just when a work was completed. 'Before the Print-Seller's', however, seems to have been painted around 1857-60.

Let us look at this small painting (33 × 25 cm/13 × 9⅞ in.) which evokes a street scene in Paris. The artist often took street scenes like this as his subject, and worked them up into paintings in his studio. This painting demonstrates the pictorial intensity later found in the works of Munch. The atmosphere is sombre and painting testifies to Daumier's ability with sombre colours.

A Painting by Toulouse-Lautrec

Henri de Toulouse-Lautrec, a descendant of one of France's noblest families and spoiled by his mother because of the physical deformity from which he suffered, lived a short but intense life. He died an alcoholic at the age of thirty-seven, leaving behind a considerable body of work. I have chosen one of his less well-known portraits, entitled *'Hélène Vary'*, which he painted in 1888.

This painting, measuring 74.5 × 49 cm (29⅜ × 19¼ in.), was executed on card. Lautrec liked to work on this support because he could paint on it directly, without having to prepare the surface first. The paint also dried very quickly on it, to produce opaque colours similar to tempera, yet the support gave material effects similar to pastel. I have reproduced a photograph of the model Hélène Vary taken by François Gauzi next to the painting. By comparing the two works, you will note how much more life a painting has than a photograph and how much a painter can put into his work that does not come through in a photograph.

Let us look at how this work was painted. One can deduce from the brushstrokes that the painter used a flat stiff-bristled brush, probably a No. 5 or 6. Lautrec never used a

The model Hélène Vary photographed by
François Gauzi in 1888.
Henri de Toulouse-Lautrec: 'Hélène Vary'
74.5 × 49cm. (1888), Oil on cardboard.
Kunsthall, Bremen.

full heavy brush to make long strokes but worked instead with short hatching as if he were painting with pastels or pencils.

The colour of the support can almost always be seen through the paint, even when he used dark colours. If you analyse the colour of the blouse, you will note that he has used Prussian blue mixed with white as a base. Brushed on lightly, this blends with the colour of the support to create a greenish base. Then with pure Prussian blue, diluted to make it transparent, he painted in the areas in shadow with small strokes. For the places where the light hits the blouse, he added touches of white.

I have described the blouse in some detail because all the tones and colours, including those used for the face of this lovely young woman, contain some of the Prussian blue that forms the base colour of the blouse.

A very important exercise for you to try is to make circles, parallelograms, and other geometric forms with very dilute colours, in an attempt to imitate Lautrec's sketches and to try to work out the colours he used. At the same time, it will help you learn how to give volume to these objects. It is only through exercises like these that you will begin to achieve results.

'Remembrance of Sorrow' by Pellizza da Volpedo

I mentioned Giuseppe Pellizza da Volpedo briefly when I reproduced one of his still-lifes (page 54). Now I would like to tell you more about this painter for he is someone whose work I greatly admire. Born in 1868 in Volpedo, a hill town in the Alexandria region of Italy, he first studied at the Brera Academy in Milan, then went on to the Fine Arts Academy in Rome.

Dissatisfied with his professors there, he left Rome for Florence where he attended classes given by Fattori near the Fine Arts Academy. Fattori, who patiently and tenaciously watched over his students, recognized Pellizza's ability as a colourist early on, but urged him to work harder on his figure drawing. Pellizza followed his advice. During his stay in Florence, Pellizza began to grow interested in large-scale paintings which made him aware of how important it was to perfect his draughtmanship. As a result, he decided to attend the Carrara Academy in Bergamo, signing up for a course in painting with Cesare Tallone. It was with Tallone that he learned to paint full-sized figures. In 1897, four years before his death, he gave the Carrara Academy this portrait painted in

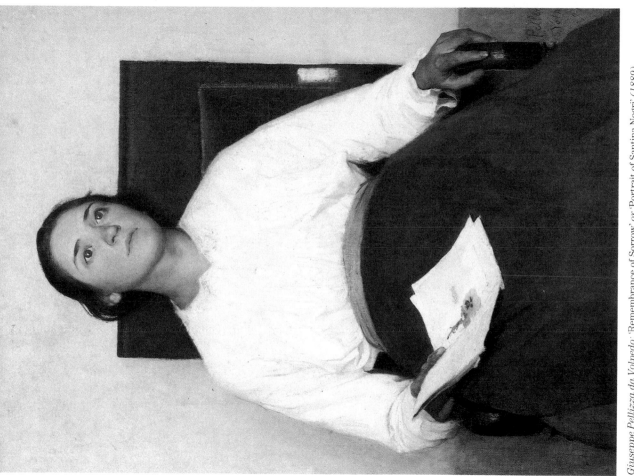

Giuseppe Pellizza da Volpedo: 'Remembrance of Sorrow' or 'Portrait of Santina Negri' (1889), 107 × 79cm. Oil on canvas. Accademia Carrara, Bergamo.

1889 and entitled *'Remembrance of Sorrow'* or *'Portrait of Santina Negri'* as a token of his esteem and in recognition of the training he had received there.

The painting is linked stylistically to the European realist movement; it is based on a solid preparatory drawing and soft colours are used in its execution. Great care and concern are shown in the portrayal of the woman, whose sad pensive expression is echoed in every detail of the composition from the wood of the armchair to the pressed pansy in the book.

I personally watched over the reproduction of the painting and its printing for this book, yet, good as it is, it still cannot convey the emotion that one feels when looking at the original, something that is true of all works of art. That is why I advise you to visit museums and galleries as often as you can.

The life and works of Pellizza da Volpedo offer us an important lesson: one must never stop learning, never stop working. One must paint for the love of painting – not for fame.

Painting is a demanding art. You must paint and draw all the time, devote every spare minute to it, and never, ever give up. And when you think you have reached your goal, you will only be halfway there.

A Famous Academician, Cesare Tallone

Cesare Tallone (1853-1919) was one of those rare academicians who left a strong mark on his students.

He studied in Milan at the Brera Academy, then went to Rome in the early 1880s where he shared an apartment with Antonio Mancini, who had some influence on his work. In 1885 he was appointed a professor at the Carrara Academy in Bergamo where one of his students was Pellizza da Volpedo. In 1898, he went to the Brera Academy teaching, among others, Carlo Carra.

Tallone was, above all, a landscape and portrait painter. Many of his portraits are life-sized. We have reproduced here of his works, 'Portrait of Angelo Galimberti'.

Note the feeling of volume and the modelling he has given to the figure. You might find it a helpful exercise to re-create this painting. Do not give up or stop trying just because you do not achieve perfect results the first time. Do not worry that you will become only an imitator of other works by copying something. Studying and reproducing great works helps you to build a solid base from which you can develop your own style.

Cesare Tallone: 'Portrait of Angelo Galimberti' (1910). Oil on canvas. Civica Galleria d'Arte Moderna, Milan.

'Portrait of Luisella'

I did this portrait of my wife (overleaf) in 1979 and as with so many other studies I have done, I started out using one technique and ended using another.

So that my wife would not have to pose for too long a time, I sketched the portrait directly on to a canvas. I had just prepared this canvas with glue and it was not yet completely dry. I then outlined the contour of the figure with a brush dipped in powdered raw umber. The result was interesting, so I decided to continue using powdered colours over the glue, mixing the colours on my palette first, just as if they were paints. Of course, when working with glue like this, you must be careful not to damage the palette and you must also watch out for gusts of air that might blow the powder around.

I worked with the powders until the coating was dry, and then I continued with oils.

Here is what to do if you would like to copy this portrait. Begin in the centre with the face, and separate the clearly defined areas of light and shadow. To do this, mix yellow ochre with an equal amount of zinc white and a little vermilion and spread this over the side of the face in the light. To paint the side of the face in shadow, add a little

104

ultramarine and the same amount of burnt umber to your base colour.

For the hair, use the lighter flesh tone with a good amount of burnt sienna added to it. The dressing gown is a mixture of Prussian blue, a little ultramarine and white. If you have worked the colour over the area using small brushstrokes (by that I do not mean delicate strokes but short strokes, the way one would apply paint to a wall) and if you have finished your painting in one sitting, you will have achieved a coloured image that may remind you of one of Daumier's figures.

The background was painted with two different shades of the same colour, raw umber with a little yellow ochre and white for the lower part, and the same colour with more white for the upper section.

Now let us return to the face. The colour of the shadow on the right cheek is the same colour as that used for the part of the cheek in direct light; only a little cerulean has been added to it. For the shadow created by the fringe, you must add a little burnt umber and a very small amount of cerulean to the lighter colour of the face.

The shadow on the chin is the same colour as the umber of the forehead but the one on the chin has just a little more white and cerulean added to it.

For the shading of the hair, try to distinguish between the variations of red, yellow or blue and add these tones to your base colour. Brush them on in wide strokes, then smudge them slightly with a dry brush. Follow this procedure for the dressing gown.

If instead of copying my work, you are able to work directly from nature by painting a friend, your exercise will be even more useful and will certainly give you more satisfaction.

'Self-portrait' by Gianni Maimeri

At the beginning of this century, many new trends sprang up around the so-called avant-garde movement. All of them, rightly or wrongly, turned their backs on figure drawing and looked to other subjects. Some painters, however, stayed in the background of this storm and just painted whatever they wanted to paint. Gianni Maimeri was among them. In 1930, he exhibited a group of his works at the salon of *Giornale dell'Arte* and Carlo Carra called him 'one of those rare beings for whom painting is the fruit of study and love, someone who shows an appropriate concept of art and a genuine awareness of its nature'.

Gianni Maimeri: 'Self-portrait' (1932), 40 × 50cm. Oil on canvas. Private Collection, Milan.

One of the most important things – in fact, almost *the* most important thing – to learn when painting a portrait is where to place the shadows. Look carefully at Maimeri's painting.

The light seems to be coming from a small window above and behind him; the warm tones of the canvas suggest the presence of a small lamp. Only a small part of his hair is highlighted; the rest of it is almost the same shade as the background. The background has probably been painted with a mixture of Vandyke brown, raw umber and a little white. Using that as a base, he has added yellow ochre and white for the hair that is highlighted, and for the rest of it in the shadows, Vandyke brown, raw umber and a little ultramarine.

I would guess that the flesh tones are a mixture of yellow ochre, white and a touch of vermilion, while the warmer areas have a little burnt earth added and the cooler areas, a little blue mixed in.

This portrait reminds me of the following famous self-portrait by Courbet with which Maimeri must have been familiar.

'Man with a Pipe' by Gustave Courbet

Gustave Courbet was born on 10th January, 1819 in Ornans, in the heart of the Jura Mountains, to a comfortable Jacobin peasant family. In 1839, he went to Paris with the intension of studying law, but instead began to study painting in the studio of Flajoulot, a student of David, and also took lessons from Steuben, a painter of historical subjects. After that, he attended the Swiss Academy, but grew dissatisfied there and started to paint on his own, attaching himself to Corot and the group of painters who worked in the forests of Fontainebleau.

Back in Paris again after 1850, he took an active part in the discussions on the new school of 'realism'. These discussions drew together many famous personalities of the day, including Proudhon, Baudelaire and even Daumier.

In 1870, along with Daumier, he was awarded the Legion of Honour, but both refused it for political reasons. Courbet said, 'I am a republican and I refuse to accept the Legion of Honour unless it is given equally and without discrimination to an ironmonger and a minister.'

Baudelaire wrote: *It is in this respect that he (Ingres) has something in common – as paradoxical as it may seem – with the young painter M. Courbet who is also a powerful worker, with an untamed and indomitable spirit, and the results he has obtained, results which for some have more charm than those of a great master like Raphael. Politics and literature produce these vigorous temperaments, these protestants, these anti-supernaturalists, whose only legitimacy is a rather healthy spirit of reaction. Providence, presiding over the affairs of the painter, gives him as accomplices all those whom the predominant opposing ideas have either exhausted or oppressed. The difference is, the heroic sacrifice that M. Ingres has made in honour of tradition and the idea of a Raphael-like beauty, M. Courbet has accomplished with a positive, immediate, external nature. In their war of imaginations, they obey different motivations; but their two contrary fanaticisms lead them to the same sacrifice.'*

Gros-Kost, evoking the relationship between Courbet and Baudelaire, wrote, *'Courbet reproached Baudelaire for his abuse of drugs but even so he listened to the words that the poet pronounced when he was delirious or in a stupor. He took advantage of the occasion to paint the famous portrait of him in 1855 that is part of his larger composition "The Studio".'*

Among the many self-portraits Courbet painted, this is one he did between 1846 and 1847. The artist has given himself an ironic expression. He defies the world and seems almost to scorn his fellow man.

Look at the light, and the detailed analysis of the lines and contractions of the face. They are absolutely realistic and alive. The colour range is the same as that used by Maimeri, or rather Maimeri's portrait recalls that of Courbet.

This portrait can be used as an example to help you learn to construct the head. Find a piece of tracing paper and place it over the painting. Now trace the oval of the face and mark the axes. According to rules set down by the ancient Greeks and Romans, the head was divided into four parts. The first part starts at the top of the head and goes to the roots of the hair, the second goes to the eyebrows, the third to the base of the nose and the last to the bottom of the chin. Use that as a rule when constructing heads.

Be careful to respect the parallel lines of the movement of the eyes. Be aware, however, that there are some well-known portraits whose subjects have been painted cross-eyed intentionally, such as 'La Celestina' by Picasso which we will look at next.

Gustav Courbet: 'Man with a Pipe' *(1847). Oil on canvas. Musée Fabre, Montpellier.*

Pablo Picasso: 'La Celestina' (1903), 60 × 81cm. Oil on canvas. Private Collection, Paris.

'La Celestina' by Pablo Picasso

Picasso was a key figure in modern art. This is why I thought it would be interesting for you to copy this portrait, painted in 1903, as an exercise in painting the eye.

To make it easier, divide your work into four stages. First, draw the outline of an eye with a pencil, using a stippled line to define the shadows.

Second, fill in the background eye colour using a blend of white, raw sienna, vermilion and a little cerulean to give it a cool tone. Use very dilute colours. For the iris, mix some bistre which you will blend with a little white for the lighter parts.

Third, accentuate the parts of the eye in shadow near the tear ducts and define the pupil with a sustained bistre.

Fourth, and finally, add some white highlights to the eye, to make it look more brilliant and crystal-like.

Now, we will look at how to draw an ear. Because the position of the woman in 'La Celestina' only allows you to see one ear, we will turn instead to a painting by van Gogh.

The Ear

To practise drawing the ear, I chose this 'Portrait of a Man' by Vincent van Gogh. Un-like Picasso, van Gogh was not known for his skill in anatomical drawing, but his forceful compositions and the powerful emotion expressed in his works made up for any lack of technical ability.

When painting the ear, you must begin with a concise drawing. Then, decide on the colour you need to cover the largest surface. In van Gogh's painting, it was a mixture of yellow ochre, white and a little vermilion, with a touch of carmine added.

Initially you should experiment with only small quantities of colour on your palette. Then, if your colour looks too red, you can add a little white and ochre; if it is too ochre, add a little red; and if it is too white, add both ochre and red. The tone used for the lightest areas should also be the coolest.

Next, blend raw umber with a little bistre. Then, using large strokes and a flat brush, trace the outline.

The shadow under the earlobe can be made with burnt ochre mixed with the same colour that you used for the areas in direct light. Work with the flat brush that you used for the outline, dabbing on the shadows over the area you have just painted. Avoid going over it more than once, however, or the two colours will mix. The colour should be

111

spread in one go. It is important to keep it confined to that area so that it does not mix with other nearby colours.

Each time you go to a museum, take the time to look at the details of paintings, and note how the artist achieved different effects. This will help you learn to lay out colours on your canvas and to create special effects by superimposing tone on tone. At the beginning, however, try to work with the colours you have prepared on your palette.

The Nose
Once again, we turn to the works of the great masters – this time, to learn how to paint the nose. But, first, practise drawing many noses of different shapes and sizes, especially in profile – aquiline, turned up, bulbous, with large nostrils and small ones.

Vincent van Gogh: 'Portrait of an Actor' *(1888), 54.5 × 65cm. Rijksmuseum Kroeller-Muller, Amsterdam.*

Henri de Toulouse-Lautrec: 'Marcelle' *(1894), 46.5 × 29.5cm. Musée Toulouse-Lautrec, Albi.*

'Marcelle' by Henri de Toulouse-Lautrec

As I mentioned earlier, Toulouse-Lautrec often worked on unprepared card because he liked the spontaneous feeling this surface gave to his painting. As you can see, 'Marcelle' has been painted directly on the support, using colours diluted with turpentine.

Note that the whole composition, including the background, was quickly sketched in first, before any details were added. This is a very good preliminary step to take since it allows you to control tonal values.

Now look at the nose. To copy it, draw it first in pencil and go over your drawing with a round-tipped hair-type brush. Then outline the contours in pencil again. Now you can paint in the colours. The basic skin tone is a mixture of yellow ochre and white to which a little red should be added for the warmer tones of the nose. Finally, we come to the mouth. To learn how to paint this last feature, we will turn to a work by Gauguin.

'Madeleine Bernard' by Paul Gauguin

Gauguin, another of the great Impressionists, was a master at rendering light and also at portraying his subjects with dramatic expressions, something which had a strong impact on Edvard Munch.

Gauguin himself was an admirer of the paintings of Paul Cézanne.

The successors of Gauguin and Cézanne formed an important group at the Salon des Indépendants, where radical painters were able to exhibit their work. Gauguin was particularly fond of exotic themes. No matter who his subject was, he somehow managed to give the person an oriental air, as you can see here.

I have always found Gauguin's mouths particularly striking. In this and in many of his other paintings, the mouth is fleshy and sensual. Look at the painting closely. The upper lip is in shadow in relation to the lower lip, which is the way it would be under normal lighting conditions. If the light were to come from below, the reverse would be true.

To paint a mouth (or in this case, to copy one), mix a flesh tone of ochre, opaque zinc white and vermilion and add to it a small amount of a mixture of four parts vermilion and one part carmine. For the area in shadow, add a little raw umber or ultramarine to the basic colour, depending on the tone you want.

Paul Gauguin: 'Madeleine Bernard' *(1880), 72 × 58cm. Musée de Peinture et de Sculpture, Grenoble.*

'The Four Seasons' by Giuseppe Arcimboldo

Now it is time for you to begin putting together the details we have looked at in paintings of your own. Along with subjects taken from life, a painter should be able to create on his canvas forms and images from his imagination. The paintings of Giuseppe Arcimboldo are a typical example of the art of the imagination. Arcimboldo became famous for his incredible portraits. Clearly very attracted by the colours and shapes found in nature, he used his imagination to create completely new images. We have all looked at a cloud and seen an animal or some other object in it. The portraits on the following pages were inspired by the four seasons, with the artist interpreting each subject in a different way. Each painting has the same basic form and is distinguished only by its details.

Giuseppe Arcimboldo was born in Milan in 1527 to a noble family who, according to the biographer Paolo Morigi, dated back to the pre-Carolingian era. Here are some notes on the artist, taken from Morigi's biography.

Maximilian of Austria, who was elected king by the Romans and thereafter became emperor, invited Arcimboldo to enter his service. After some hesitation, Giuseppe accepted and in 1562 went to the court of the emperor, where Maximilian received him with full honour.'

One also finds in the writings of Gianpaolo Lomazzo, a painter, poet and art critic of the sixteenth century, a description of the paintings reproduced on the next pages.

'The museum of his Caesarian majesty the emperor Maximilian II is a remarkable one. To display his grandeur and noblesse, he asked the great painter Giuseppe Arcimboldo to decorate it, using his great ingenuity with perspective, his great skill with the art of relief and above all, his wonderful inventiveness and sense of caprice, which have made him unique in the world. What he has done is to paint the forms of the four elements. And he has portrayed the four seasons as figures of men, each made with objects connected with that season, for example, Spring with flowers, Summer with vegetables, Autumn with fruit and Winter with trees. Each represents an inestimable tableau. He has also painted a Janus made of objects from the entire year: the profile has aspects of Summer, the head those of Winter, the year, a serpent wrapped around the neck eating its tail.'

Giuseppe Arcimboldo: 'The Four Seasons' (1573), 72.5 × 39cm. Oil on canvas. Private Collection (formerly part of the Cornelia Collection, the Countess of Craven Hamstead Marshall).

Giuseppe Arcimboldo: 'The Four Seasons' (1573), 72.5 × 39cm. Oil on canvas. Private Collection (formerly part of the Cornelia Collection, the Countess of Craven Hamstead Marshall)

THE NUDE

Dilettante or not, every painter, no matter what his style, sooner or later looks to the nude for the greatest expressiveness.

You should always start with the head when you paint or draw a nude, because as we learned earlier, the head is the basic unit of measure for the body.

When you paint a nude, no matter what style you intend to use, always proceed in orderly stages; unfortunately this is something inexperienced painters often fail to do.

Let us see what Vasari says in *Lives of the Artists*:

'Having made one's preparation, that is, mixing the shades to be used when working with oils, distemper, or frescos, one should go back over the lines, placing in the right spots the light and dark colours and halftones, along with the variations of halftones and light colours, that is to say, the different mixtures of the three base colours, the light, medium and dark tones. Each can be inferred from the preliminary sketches or other drawings carried out before undertaking a work of this type. In the project, the

things put down on paper should be balanced, the drawing carefully studied, and everything should be rendered with confidence and a creative spirit. In painting, putting the work on paper consists of deciding where to place each figure, organizing the spaces to the satisfaction of the eye to avoid badly proportioned figures and dividing up the spaces and forms. Now all of this is achieved through practice, drawing from nature or using models suitable for what one intends to do. I will say it once more: no project can be good if it does not proceed from constant recourse to drawing from nature and the study of the great masters and ancient statues. Studying the nude and working with a live model, be it a man or a woman, is essential; such an exercise, repeated constantly, fixes in the mind the configuration of the muscles of the torso, the back, the legs, the arms, the knees, and, in more depth, the skeleton: this way, one will be able to draw from memory the exact disposition of the body in every position. The study of anatomical models allows one to learn the position of the bones, the muscles, the nerves and all the elements of anatomy and to place the limbs and muscles of the human body correctly.

A Nude by Edward Hopper

Edward Hopper (1882-1967), the American painter and engraver, attended the New York School of Art from 1905 to 1910 and then travelled to Europe where he met many French painters. When he returned to America, he spent eight years working on engravings, then turned to painting. In an exhibition of his work in 1927 he revealed himself as one of the most representative realist painters of modern America. His subjects offers a critical study of American society, particularly small-town life.

There is almost a metaphysical stupor in the silence that Hopper is able to suggest in his canvases. This atmosphere prevails in the work I have reproduced here, 'Hotel Room ', painted in 1931.

The hotel room has that characteristic anonymous atmosphere that one still finds in certain hotels dating from the 1930s. The large white wall and the grey corner in the foreground are in cool neutral tones. It is worth noting that white is the absence of colour and bistre grey is the sum of all the colours.

Edward Hopper: 'Hotel Room' (1931), 152.4 × 165.1cm. Oil on canvas. Thyssen Bornemisza Collection, Lugano.

121

Try this exercise along these lines.

Prepare a canvas or a piece of wood panel the same size as the Hopper canvas, 152.4 × 165.1 cm (60 × 65 in.). Tape some tracing paper over the reproduction on the next page with adhesive tape (the kind that you can remove easily without damaging the paper). Using an HB pencil, first outline the square framework, then very lightly draw a grid on your paper and finally carefully trace the whole composition.

On your canvas, draw in another grid very lightly with a pencil, using the same number of squares as the one reproduced here. Then it will be easy to transfer your drawing on to the canvas, using the lines of the grid as reference points. When you have finished, move on to the painting itself, laying out your colours on a large palette.

For the background white, mix white with some bistre (if you were to use only pure white, the effect would be too dazzling) and brush it on with a firm bristle brush.

The same white, to which a little yellow ochre has been added, should be used for the curtain, while the yellow part of the wall should be made of yellow ochre mixed with about ten per cent white. Prepare some bistre blended with a little white for the grey

band on the left. For all the woods, use a base colour of burnt umber or Vandyke brown, adding a little yellow ochre for the light areas and a little raw umber for the darker areas.

The colour of the bedspread is white with a touch of carmine; the coverlet at the foot of the bed is carmine with equal amounts of vermilion and white. The lighter of the two pieces of luggage is raw sienna mixed with a little raw umber. The darker suitcase is

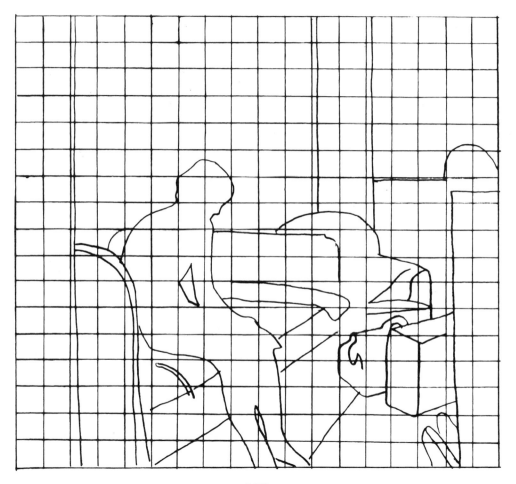

123

bistre with raw umber. These same colours are also used for the shoes, the hat and the darker part of the wall in the background; to this last colour, add a little blue.

The flesh tones of the figure come from mixing yellow ochre, white and a little vermilion for the areas that are highlighted; for the half-tones, add some raw umber to the basic colour. Natural umber is also used for the face.

For the greens, mix ultramarine and yellow until you have a balanced shade. Add emerald green to make it more brilliant and use white to set the tone of the painting.

Dull green is obtained by adding ultramarine blue and a little carmine to the previous green.

These colours are the basic colours which can be warmed up or cooled down, or made lighter or darker for those areas where there are variations of light.

'The Great Bathers' by Paul Cézanne

This outstanding composition, which the artist apparently worked on over seven years, from 1898 to 1905, has been called 'the masterpiece of Cézanne's architectonic fantasy'. Against a background of colour, each figure finds its place within the architecture of the whole.

The beauty of this composition, with its nudes and splendid colours, struck Henry Moore very forcefully. It is not often that one artist expresses such a positive response to the work of another. Moore wrote:

'I was at college and had begun my first year at university when I was filled with a desire to see the original paintings by Cézanne. I spoke to my professor about it and asked him if I could go to Paris for a week. He replied, "Yes, and I will even give you a letter of recommendation." In fact, he wrote one for me to give to Maillol but my great shyness prevented me from using it. I arrived at the master's door and thought, "he will probably be working and not want to be disturbed." So I left.

'Anyway, I went to see the Pellerin collection. There, I felt great emotion when I saw Cézanne's canvas, with its triangular composition of bathers. In it, the nudes seem to be in perspective, stretched out on the ground as if they are sculptures, fashioned from rock. For me, it was the same as seeing

Paul Cézanne: 'The Great Bathers' (1898-1905), 208 × 251cm. Oil on canvas. Wilstach Collection, Philadelphia Museum of Art.

Chartres cathedral.

'The way I look at it, Cézanne, in this kind of composition, was in constant competition with all the things he admired, trying to put everything he saw in them. With some of his work, he wanted to learn how to resolve and even reduce all his problems into one. To do this, he risked everything he knew about painting.

'I do not like absolute perfection. I think that each of us should struggle to accomplish what he does not know how to do rather than to do only what comes easily. Another reason why I fell in love with this painting is that he has portrayed my favourite kind of woman in it. It would be very simple for me to translate into sculpture each individual figure. These are not young women but mature, corpulent, robust women – real women! Such vitality . . . with backs almost like gorillas, flat and ordinary, but leading to a romantic idea of woman. And that is Cézanne – ready to struggle against everything he admires, against the old masters. Impressionism did not satisfy him. He said, "I want to make Impressionism an art for museums," which at the time it was not. When Cézanne went to museums and saw the Rubens, the El Gre-cos, and the Tintorettos there, he realized that there was something missing in Impressionism, a certain fullness, a certain grandeur, and depth. And thus, his life became a giant struggle based on broadening his own horizons and those of painting and art in general.'

Let us look now at the technique used by Cézanne in this remarkable painting. Over the years he used oil paints that were more and more diluted so that he was able to achieve effects similar to those produced by watercolours.

In this particular painting, he used to advantage the palette-knife technique – which he executed here using not a knife but a wide flat brush – and very dilute colours that were brushed on in short strokes, leaving patches of white (the natural colour of the canvas) between them. I have always thought that the description 'a mosaic of colour' was appropriate for this painting because the way Cézanne distributes colour distantly recalls the technique of mosaics.

If you decide to follow this method, remember that the background is painted not with one single colour but rather with a variety of colours taken from the tones of the base colour, even on a small surface.

Cézanne frequently worked with the palette knife. This technique is not difficult and the results can be very satisfying. However, a painting done with a palette knife inevitably has a heavy layer of paint on it, so the support should be suitably prepared beforehand. The ready-to-use canvases found in artists' suppliers are not suitable for this technique. To prepare a canvas, you should use linseed oil mixed with a little turpentine so that the coating also gives the canvas a bit of colour. Paint spread with a knife allows you to accentuate the illusion of volume by actually creating a thicker surface.

When the background is ready, mix your paints on your palette and, with the knife, spread a single layer of colour on to the canvas. Do this as confidently as if you were using a brush. Then, delicately superimpose a second colour over it, otherwise the one on the bottom will reappear.

If you want to mix two colours, go over the canvas from top to bottom several times very lightly with the palette knife, until you get the mix you want.

Later on, we will look in detail at how to work with the palette knife. Cézanne was a master of the technique and set an example for later artists to follow.

'Nude in the Bath' by Pierre Bonnard

Every painting, whether a still-life, a landscape, a portrait or a nude, is the result of an artist's creativity, the fruit of his invention.

To find new and personal subjects to paint is simple. All you need to do is to look around you, as if you were seeing through the lens of a camera, and choose some particular feature which will serve as a source of inspiration for your painting. It is that simple.

Sometimes, though, the simplest things are the most difficult to understand and are therefore neglected or avoided.

Toulouse-Lautrec and Pierre Bonnard found inspiration in everyday life. When they saw a face in the crowd or a figure that struck them, they made a rapid sketch on a sheet of paper or, as did Bonnard, in a simple pocket diary.

Often a famous painting starts from such beginnings, as was the case with Bonnard's *Nude in the Bath*.

The artist probably drew it while he was sitting in a café or on a park bench; most likely, the image just appeared in his mind. The only model the painter used was his wife, Marthe. With merely a few strokes of his pencil, he sketched the whole scene. He probably had his model work at the same time every day so that he could use natural light to advantage.

The range of colours that Bonnard used was developed through observation and also through an exaggeration of the effects of light. This canvas, with its predominant yellows and blues, has a certain Mediterranean warmth to it.

If you get used to observing and analysing the variations of warm and cool colours on the surface of objects that you paint, you will quickly be able to reproduce them.

Try to analyse for yourself the colours that Bonnard has used in this painting. The wall in the background, for example, is a play of yellow and violet that is broken by a white light in the centre. Be careful though, because this white light contains traces of red, yellow and blue in tiny amounts, which give the usually neutral white some colour.

Now look at the two yellows. The one on the left of the canvas is mixed with a little orange. The window frame is yellow mixed with a little bistre, and by alternating with red and blue tones, it gives the effect of two different areas, indoors and out.

The yellow on the right, placed between white and reddish violet, is in the same range as the yellow on the left but it has more

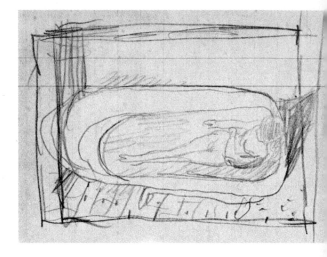

Pierre Bonnard: 'Nude in the Bath' *and preliminary study (1935), 147 × 93cm. Oil on canvas. Petit Palais, Paris.*

orange added to it, giving it a warmer tone that makes it stand out.

We can discuss the blue-violet on the left and the red-violet on the right in the same way. On a colour wheel these two colours are not very far apart, but the blue on the left is cooler and gives a sense of depth. The darker blue beneath the yellow gives the illusion of an angle while the red violet on the right comes forward.

128

Moving on to the bathtub, we see that the rim was painted using all three colours in succession, blue on the left, white in the centre and yellow on the right. All the other colours are lightened with white and less red is brushed on. Contrast is produced with white horizontal strokes over the yellow background and by the small white washcloth on the left, whose role is also to define the boundary between the blue and the grey-bistre of the background.

The interior of the bathtub and the figure immersed in the water are painted with variations of the colours used for the background. Bistre is the base colour of the water. The blue-violet strokes create the impression of reflecting water, while the darker flesh tones come from mixing yellow ochre, a little vermilion and white. The short pink, blue and yellow strokes not only give the body volume but also add a feeling of transparency to the water. Just below the breasts, the warmer flesh tone has more ochre in it.

The white blueness of the water covering the right breast is reflected in the face. Behind the head, one finds a white that has more grey in it than the central colour. Just behind it is a greyed yellow, then a long band of almost pure white. This same white appears in the triangle formed by the small mat in the lower part of the painting.

The floor is a combination of cobalt blue mixed with a little white on a bistre ground. On the tiles on the right you can see the yellow reflection of the window going under the old-fashioned bathtub with its clawed feet.

Pierre Bonnard was born in Fontenay-aux-Roses in 1867. He left his law studies to take up an artistic career as a draughtsman of posters and an illustrator of books, which he pursued until 1947.

He reached the peak of his expressive powers at the beginning of this century and worked constantly for the next forty years, maintaining the same style in spite of the various movements that sprang up around him, including the avant-garde.

In the 1920's he moved to Provence, partly because of his wife's ill-health. There, his canvases were filled with the lively colours of the Mediterranean. Sunny landscapes gave way to small paintings of family life or sun-filled interiors where bright cobalt blue tiles reflected the luminous power of the rooms where his female nudes appear, a subject that was one of his favourites in later life.

'Nude in the Bath' is from a series of nudes, painted in 1937.

LANDSCAPES

Even though landscape painting has its origins in antiquity and over the centuries has been subjected to many different rules and interpretations (the realist perspectives of the Renaissance, the fantastic or idealistic scenes of the sixteenth century, and later, naturalism), it was not until the Impressionists and the Pointillists that artists actually painted outdoors. Until that time, painting had always been carried out inside, in the studio, with the artists working from notes and sketches.

By painting outdoors, artists were able to capture the extraordinary effect of sunlight on objects. This is why their paintings are so much more alive and striking than those painted in the studio.

I suggest that you begin by painting a landscape when the countryside is in full bloom, if possible on a cloudy day. This will provide you with a more uniform light, without sharply defined shadows and bright sunlight. Work with a small format using a wide, firm, hair-type brush. This will prevent you from trying to put in too much detail and help you to focus your attention on large masses. Remember that details should be added last. Paint the large volumes first to lay out the overall composition, otherwise you will find it hard to define the different tones.

To learn how to frame your landscape, you might try using a system employed by the early photographers. It consists of making a black frame, smaller than but in proportion to your canvas, from a piece of cardboard. For example, if your canvas measures 35 × 50 cm (11¾ × 13¾ in.) make a frame that is one-tenth that size. Hold the frame at arm's length so that you can see at a glance the view that you want to paint. Then move it to the right or to the left, up or down, until you find just the right composition.

There is another kind of frame or 'perspective frame' that a landscape painter ought to have, which is also constructed in proportion to your support. To make it, you will need some wooden boards, some small nails and twine. Make a series of holes around the edge of your wood. Then, assemble your wood according to the drawing below. By winding string around nails stuck in the holes, you can lay out the diagonals and the median lines of your composition and make a similar series of light marks on your canvas with a pencil. Nail the frame to a long pole and stick the pole firmly in the ground so that the frame itself is at eye level. Then you can choose a composition and, looking at it through the frame, use the lines as reference points to transfer what you see on to your canvas.

When you are ready to work, take a piece of plywood, give it a background colour of burnt umber heavily diluted with some white

spirit, and off you go!

I painted the scene reproduced for you here during a short thunderstorm.

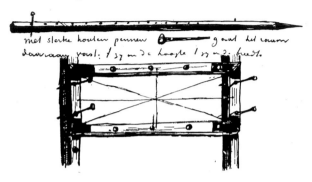

If you would like to do a similar sketch, start with a quick drawing made with a very soft pencil. Pay particular attention to the greens when you mix your paints. They are difficult to get just right, and beginners often make them too yellow. You should start with ultramarine blue or Prussian blue and add small amounts of yellow until you get the right shade. Always have a little bistre prepared and close at hand to add to the green when you need a darker shade.

Once you have finished your drawing, begin by brushing on a wide swath of green in the foreground (this is also the warmest

area of the painting). This green is made by mixing emerald, a little Veronese green, cadmium yellow and a little zinc white. Before you start working with the other colours, glance quickly several times at the colours you have mixed on the palette and then back to the landscape. This way of constantly comparing colours will help you to get the right green, almost as if you were superimposing one colour on top of the other, like a piece of film. It is an optical illusion you may have to try several times before you get satisfactory results.

For the green in the middle ground, add a little white to the green you already have. For the foliage of the trees in the background, prepare a well-balanced shade of bistre and add to it a touch of emerald green and white. The shadows and the bushes under the trees can also be painted with the same colour. Now mix some emerald green with a little red, add a little of

the colour you used for the bushes and a little white and use this for the foliage of the trees in the foreground. The tree trunks should be the same colour as you used to coat the wood support and the sky very white with a touch of bistre. If the bistre is well-balanced, the finished sky will be a silvery colour.

'Morning' by Antonio Fontanesi

The landscape painter Antonio Fontanesi was born in Reggio Emilia in 1818 and studied art there under the direction of P. Minghetti. In 1848, he moved to Turin, drawn by the ideals of the *Risorgimento*, and joined the regiments of the House of Savoy. Two years later, he arrived in Geneva where he discovered the paintings of Alexandre Calame, a well-known landscape artist from Piedmont. Fontanesi made several trips around Europe and he was acquainted with the best-known schools of contemporary painting.

In 1855 in Paris, he became interested in Corot and the Barbizon school. In 1861 he took part in the First Italian Fair inaugurated in Florence. At this exhibition, one could find just about anything – there were livestock and agricultural products, as well as the latest scientific and technological discoveries. Paintings were also on show and the occasion brought together many Italian painters. Fontanesi wrote to a friend about it saying, *'Florence is one big party, the hotels are filled, everyone is very animated and there is an atmosphere of excitement and gaiety about the town. Moving among such beautiful things, the night intoxicates me and I can't sleep.'*

At the exhibition, he met Christian Banti and they became good friends. In 1866 when Fontanesi found himself penniless in London, with no way of returning to Italy, it was to Banti that he turned, and it was Banti who rescued him. Banti also helped him by commissioning paintings from him while he was waiting for a position at the Academy at Lucca.

In 1863, Fontanesi again took part in the New Italian Exhibition, submitting the painting reproduced on the opposite page. The work was not for sale, however; it was one of the works that Banti had commissioned.

In 1869, he finally settled permanently in Turin where he was given the chair of landscape painting and made the director of engraving at the Albertina Academy. The influence of his European experiences, both

Antonio Fontenesi: 'Morning' *(1856-8), 32 × 21.5cm. Oil on canvas. Museo Civico, Turin.*

French and English, can be seen in this landscape, entitled '*Morning*'. Let us see how he painted it.

The trees in the foreground are in shadow while those in the middle ground and background are in the light. This creates the optical illusion that their sombre mass is leaping forward instead of sinking back.

Do not be surprised that such optical illusions are used in painting. Take advantage of these visual tricks developed by the great masters and learn from them.

If you extend the axes of the two tree trunks, they form a triangle. The sky occupies two and a half times the space of the meadow. The trees in the middle ground have been painted with bistre mixed with terre verte and a little emerald green. The same colours plus ultramarine blue and a little white have been used for the trees in the foreground, to make them stand out against the middle ground.

The woods in the background were painted with a mixture of the green that was used for the trees in the foreground plus ultramarine and white. For the sky, add a large quantity of white to the colour of the trees. The effect of this play of colours, suggesting light and depth, gives a strong feeling of peace and harmony. One can find an atmosphere like this at the beginning of summer just at dawn in the Lombardy countryside, when the sun has barely risen above the trees and the stifling heat has not yet turned the day hazy, dulling the colours.

'Hotel on the Lake at Molveno'

Using more or less the same range of colours as Fontanesi used in his canvas, I painted this storm on the lake, with a flock of crows in the foreground. My support was untreated plywood that had been coated with very dilute umber.

The lake in the foreground was painted using the same colours as the sky, a blend of white with a little bistre. To paint the warmer area on the right, I added a little yellow to this base colour and to paint the cooler area on the left, I added a little ultramarine blue.

For the part of the lake nearest the shore, add emerald green and cerulean blue, to depict the reflections of the plants in the shallow water.

After you have covered the canvas with your base colours, use a flat brush to paint a little white over the surface of the lake to suggest the movement of the water. Work with small strokes in an irregular diagonal

pattern to give the impression of waves.

    Look at the effect of the light on the waves as they break over the small rocks and then fall again on the still water. Note carefully the circles that are formed where the water is most luminous. This should help you to work out how you yourself can achieve something similar when you paint. For the other greens, look back at what I said about the Fontanesi painting. Try to work out the colours for yourself by looking at the reproduction.

A View of Venice by Gianni Maimeri

This exercise is slightly more difficult: copying a landscape reflected in water. If a landscape seems difficult, one reflected in water is even more so.

Gianni Maimeri, the last of the great

Gianni Maimeri: 'Venice' preliminary drawing (1947). Pencil on paper. Private Collection, Milan.

school of Lombardy painters, was an excellent landscapist. Notice the care with which he made his preparatory sketch. His professional skill is also revealed in the preliminary stages of the finished canvas, in his pencil drawings, notes, watercolours and gouaches,

Gianni Maimeri: 'Venice' (1947), 25 × 16cm. Oil on canvas. Private Collection, Milan.

and in the small rough sketches for his oil paintings.

Let us analyse this view of Venice. The area on the right is painted in neutral grey tones; the area on the left is in ochre, yellow and white, another neutral tone; only the red brick bridge interrupts this monochromatic colour scheme.

All the greys on the right have been achieved by mixing zinc white and bistre with a little ochre and umber. All the yellow ochres on the left have been achieved with untinted ochre and white; the dark variations have raw umber added.

Untinted grey was also used for the contours of the bridge, while the bricks were painted with pure burnt ochre, straight from the tube.

The sky is white with a little cerulean blue added. For the reflections, take the colours from the top half of the painting and repeat them where they are reflected in the water. Finish by painting the vibrating light on the water, using small dark strokes of burnt ochre, on the blue reflection of the sky.

'The Park of Schönbrunn' by Gustav Klimt

The painter Gustav Klimt was one of the founders of the Vienna Secessionist movement in 1897 and although he was not its central figure, he has become one of its best known. Klimt did not enjoy talking either about himself or his ideas on art, and he liked writing about them even less. For this reason, I found very interesting this brief passage taken from one of the rare pieces in which he did write something about himself. *'I paint and draw well; I believe this and others also say so, but in fact, I am not sure it is true. I know only two things that are certain: first, there are no self-portraits of me. I do not interest myself as a subject – others inspire me more, especially women, and there are other subjects that inspire me far more still. I am convinced that there is nothing particularly interesting about me as a subject. I am just a painter who works every day painting a few figures and landscapes and some portraits. Second, my words and my writing are not worth much, especially if I must talk about myself or my work. For anyone who wants to know more about me, at least as an artist, the only worthwhile way is to look attentively at my works to find out who I am and what I want.'*

Gustav Klimt: 'The Park at Schönbrunn' *(1916), 110 × 110cm. Private Collection, Graz.*

Klimt is best known for his beautiful paintings of women. But, as he himself wrote, he also painted landscapes and gardens filled with poetry.

He had a very personal way of painting that reminds me of the Pointillist technique. In this view of the Schönbrunn Park, painted in 1916, the trees in the background were rendered with short strokes following the shape of the leaves, over a light green background. The violet over green gives it an unusual effect. The green comes from mixing yellow and blue, and the violet from mixing blue and red: yellow and violet are complementary colours, as are red and green. Placed side by side, these colours create an effect of luminosity.

The feeling of depth is obtained by using flat tints mixed with tones that gradually grow cooler as they move towards the background. The composition is given an original and unique frame. One glimpses the horizon line behind the trees; the small lake forms an open angle at the point of which lies a statue half hidden by the trunk of the tree just in front of it.

The sky in the upper right is a blue and white rectangle cut by the sinuous movement of clouds. The sky, reflected in the stagnant water, is made larger, as is the green reflected there. Notice the variations in the green reflections: a strip coming from the left is reflected as if a gust of wind had rippled the surface of the water on the right. To be a good landscapist you must learn to observe the phenomena of nature: the sun covered by a cloud, the colour of shadows, the instability of reflections in water, snow, and so on.

Reflections in the Water by Claude Monet

Claude Monet was born in Paris in 1840 and spent his childhood and youth in Le Havre. He began drawing as a boy and his first teacher was Eugène Boudin who inspired in him a love of painting outdoors. It was Boudin who encouraged him to move to Paris. There in 1859 Monet attended the Swiss Academy where one of his fellow students was Pissarro. After military service and a short stay in Le Havre, he went back to Paris. In the studio of Gleyre he met Renoir, Bazille and Sisley with whom he developed strong friendships. With them, he moved in fashionable Parisian circles and became familiar with, and delighted in, Manet's paintings. His first Impressionist works date

Claude Monet: 'Bathers at la Grenouillère' *(1869), 73 × 92cm. National Gallery, London.*

from the 1860s. These are landscapes painted in Paris, in the forests of Fontainebleau and along the banks of the Seine. It was his painting of 1874, *'Impression, Sunrise'*, that gave the name 'Impressionism' to the painting of that period and style.

Having attained a certain degree of success, he moved to Giverny where he remained until his death in 1926.

The subject that is most often depicted in Monet's works is that of water and its reflections. The painting I have reproduced for you is *'Bathers at La Grenouillère'*, painted in 1869 while Monet was visiting Renoir in Bougival along the Seine. As you look at it, try to imagine what the artist was thinking as he painted it.

My First Impressionist Attempt: Portocanale

In 1976 I tried to get the feeling of light found in Impressionist paintings into my own abstract paintings; my canvases, in spite of everything, were very colourful.

Of course, to capture the light of the Impressionists, in theory as well as in practice, one must first of all paint well figuratively. But, the next consideration is the palette.

This was my first attempt and as you can see, I was not completely successful. I had the right technique but not the right colours. I should have used more intense shades of blue – an Impressionist would not have used such grey tones. The colours of the boats should have been more brilliant, the yellow ochres should have had more cadmium yellow added to them, and I should have added touches of pure vermilion to the burnt earth tones. Now, I know how to manage these colours better and some of my figurative works can be considered Impressionist. But, of course, they are only studies and should be judged as such.

Remember these lessons and the advice I have given you for they will help you to feel more confident about your work. I advise you not to throw away the canvases that do not work; they will help you remember the errors you made and keep you from repeating them.

I will finish my lessons on landscape painting here, but they are only an attempt to get you started. You must go on yourself, learning to express through painting what you feel as you watch a sunset or a boat bobbing on the waves. If you succeed in expressing in your painting not just what you see but also what you feel, you will be happy.

145

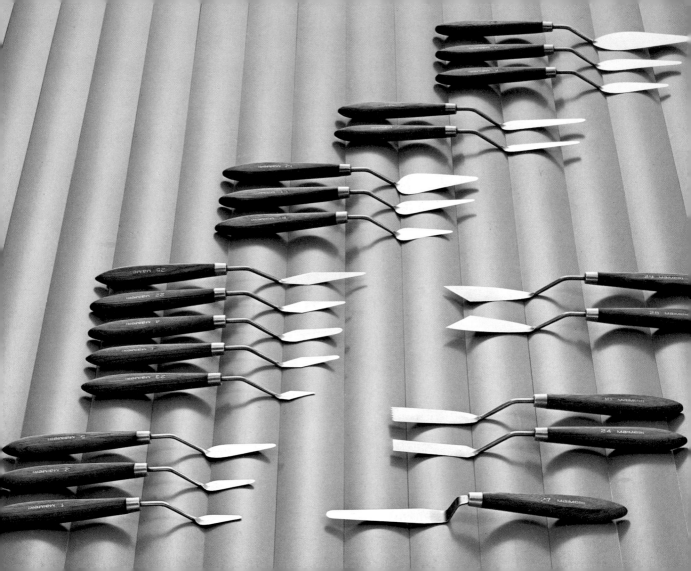

PAINTING WITH A PALETTE KNIFE

The palette knife is an invaluable tool in painting. You can use it to mix colours when there is too much paint to blend with a brush alone, and to clean your palette once you have finished working. Finally, it can be used in a different way: to create the painting itself.

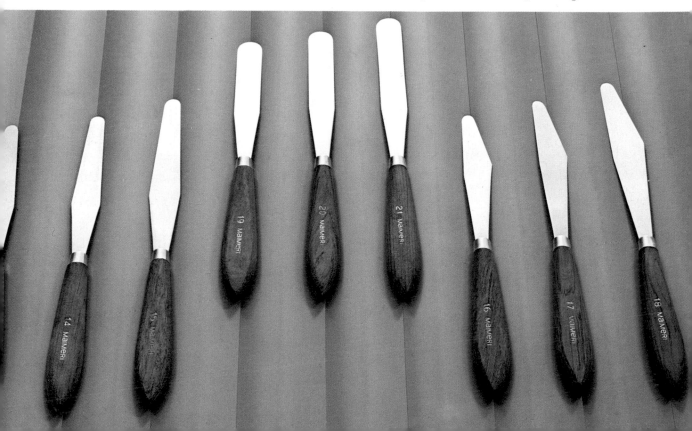

A painter usually begins to work with a palette knife when he is trying to express something beyond what he can achieve with a brush, in terms of form and volume. It is an attempt to add another expressive dimension to his work.

To create relief through colour one must work with both the thickness of the paint and a process called synthesizing or optical mixing. We will look at how the latter works. Take, for example, a poppy. If you look at the

light red with the dark red. You have synthesized the two colours into an 'optical mixture'. To get such a synthesis on the palette, we will take our palette knife and mix the light red with the dark red. This gives us a pictorial synthesis.

If we then use the palette knife to paint the flower itself, the impressions produced on the canvas will be quite different from brush strokes. The impressions depend on which shape of knife is used and the way the

first picture, you will be able to distinguish a lighter and a darker area. Therefore we will mix a light red and a dark red on the palette. Look at the poppy again, this time with half-closed eyes: your eye will blend the

instrument is held. The simplest way to hold the palette knife is to keep it flat, spreading the paint as if you were spreading butter on a piece of bread.

Certainly the impressions and the varying

thicknesses of paint that a palette knife produces are unique and individual. It is, however, not a technique that allows you to express details. Let me give you some examples of what you can do with this tool.

If you hold the knife at a 45-degree angle (figure 1), take a pure, undiluted colour straight from the tube and spread it on the canvas, you will get an effect similar to that in figure 2. On the other hand, if you dilute

the colour with a little turpentine, you will get an effect like the one in figure 3.

If you use the point of the knife (as shown in figure 4), you will get the effects you see in figure 5. If you start with pure colour, as in

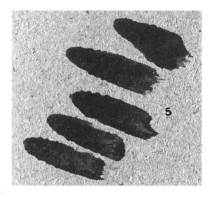

figure 2, and pass a clean knife over it, putting some pressure in your movement, you will get lines of the kind you see in figure 6. Do not hesitate to work with a palette knife;

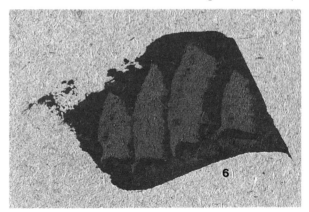

think of it as one more brush. But remember, try to synthesize your colours first.

Let us look at how some of the great painters have used this technique.

An Exercise with Camille Pissarro

The first work we will look to for inspiration as we begin our exercise with the palette knife is a still-life painted by Pissarro in 1867.

Pissarro was one of the most famous Impressionist painters. Born in the French Antilles in 1830, he was sent to complete his studies in Paris when he was just a boy. When he returned to the Antilles, he worked for his father for a short time and then left that job to start painting. In 1855, he left his family and the Antilles and moved to France.

One of the first painters he met in Paris was Corot, whom he admired a great deal, although he was never to become one of Corot's students. Instead he enrolled at the Académie des Beaux-Arts and later he attended the Swiss Academy where he met Monet and Cézanne. During the first few years of his stay in Paris, however, his closeness to Corot had a strong influence on his work. Although he eventually began to pull away from Corot and towards realism,

Pissarro was fascinated by Corot's use of the palette knife. As a result, Pissarro tried the technique himself, executing several works with the knife, including the one we have reproduced here.

In 1866, he joined his friend Cézanne in Pontoise and gave him 'some impressionist lessons'. Around 1870, he spent a short period in London because of the Prussian invasion of France, and then returned to the Antilles for a few years, setting up house in the country. Even there, however, he did not lose touch with the Parisian art world.

In 1874, he was one of the participants in the First Impressionist Exhibition, and in fact he became the only artist to take part in all the exhibitions held by the group.

In 1885, he met Seurat and Signac and was attracted to their new technique of Pointillism, but he did not continue to use Pointillism for long, deeming it too 'scientific'.

By 1896, he was back in Paris. There, in spite of serious difficulties with his eyesight, he continued to work until his death in 1903.

In his final days, unable to work outdoors, Pissarro painted a series of soft vibrant Parisian cityscapes seen through a window. Georges Leconte gives us this last image of the artist. '*One could see him morning and*

evening, an old man with a long white beard, standing by the window in front of his easel, his palette in hand, a beret on his head, and a sharp yet serene expression on his face.'

The balanced composition, the peaceful delicacy of the light that is found in the landscapes of this artist, can also be seen in this still-life, which I suggest you copy.

Look for a composition like Pissarro's and then arrange your objects as closely as possible to those in the original.

Let us look at the colours he used. First, observe the background. There, just above the tablecloth, there is a dark strip, painted in Vandyke brown mixed with a little ultramarine blue to cool down the base colour. The rest of the wall was rendered with raw sienna mixed with a small amount of the colour used for the strip and some white.

The palette knife is a kind of trowel held by the painter at a 45-degree angle (see the example on page 149). The base colour of the background, which gives an impression of relief made by the strokes of the palette knife, is lightened by adding different amounts of white, according to the degree of light falling in a particular place.

To create the small reddish area in the upper left of the painting, add a little burnt sienna to the base colour you prepared. The metallic colour of the ladles hanging on the wall comes from a mixture of bistre and white. Continue to work with a trowel-shaped palette knife but this time use just the tip.

The shadows cast by the ladles are the same colour as the ladles themselves, but with less white added to them.

For the pitcher and the glass continue to use the ladle colour as a base, but add small white to it until you reach the desired shade.

The dominant shade in the painting is bistre: the plate is also a mixture of white and bistre. Its lower part simply has a little yellow ochre added to it, corresponding to the reflection of the apples, while the apples are a lighter shade of the background colour.

For the bread, mix a little of the colour you used for the dark strip in the background with the colour with which you painted the lighter area and add white and a little burnt sienna.

Camille Pissarro: 'Still-life' (1867), 81 × 100cm. Toledo Museum of Art, Toledo, Ohio.

A Landscape by Camille Pissarro

In this painting, 'La Roche-Guyon Square', Pissarro has again used a palette knife, this time for a landscape. Landscape painting is most suited to the palette knife, for the simple reason that it is relatively easy for the artist to build up thick layers of paint over a large surface.

Pissarro was a very important figure for the young painters of his day. Many of them went to Pontoise to see him. Among them, as we have seen, was Cézanne. Pissarro always had great confidence in the talent of his friend. In fact, he wrote to Antone Guillemenet, 'Our Cézanne gives me great hope and I have seen and have at home a painting of his showing extraordinary force and vigour. If, as I hope, he stays for some time in Auvers, he will surprise many artists who have condemned him rather quickly.'

Pissarro was pleased with the progress of his protégé. Often the two of them, like Monet and Renoir, would choose the same subject and work side by side. Cézanne thus learned from his friend and teacher both the technique of constructing a composition and his vision of colour.

Emile Zola was surprised by the resemblance between the paintings of Pissarro and those of Cézanne, but Pissarro replied humbly and sensibly that it was an error to believe that 'artists are the sole inventors of their style'. It is important to realize that when two artists work together an exchange inevitably occurs, and Cézanne was as aware as Pissarro of the influence each had on the another.

Pissarro's humility and generosity comes through in his correspondence with the critic Duret. In a letter, Duret wrote: 'You don't have Sisley's decorative sense or Monet's inventive eye but you possess something they don't have and that is a deep secret intuition of nature and a strength in your brushes that makes one of your beautiful paintings something absolutely definitive. If I were to give you advice, I would say, don't think about Monet or Sisley or what they do. Work for yourself and follow your own path, that of nature and rustic life. It will give you new life and with it, you, like all the great masters, will go far.'

Sensing that Duret was devaluing Monet's work to praise his own, Pissarro replied, 'Don't you think you are mistaken about

Camille Pissarro: 'La Roche-Guyon Square' (1867), 50 × 61cm. Nationalgalerie, Berlin.

Monet's talent? His is a very careful art, based on observation, and it has a completely new feeling to it; it is poetry, a harmony of true colours.'

Let us go back now to Pissarro's landscape. The painter used a special very long, flat, and flexible palette knife, about 40mm (1½ in.) wide. The colours he used are the same as those of the still-life that we just looked at, mostly earth tones and ochres. The whole painting is painted with tone over tone. You can see a little grey sky made from bistre just behind the rooftops.

Follow the technique Pissarro used in the preceding painting. Try to work out first what colours he used and how to duplicate them, testing them on your palette before applying them to the canvas.

Pissarro quickly abandoned this style of painting for one that was much more analytical, rendered with small brushstrokes, a technique that Cézanne also adopted. Pissarro and Cézanne brought an effervescence to their paintings and, for this reason, I also want you to look at a painting by Cézanne.

'The Pond at Soeurs à Osny' by Paul Cézanne

The relationship between the two painters was, as we have seen, one of great esteem and friendship, even though Cézanne was a tenacious and aggressive fighter and Pissarro was both more poetic and more methodical.

We still think of Cézanne as the real reformer of painting, but had there been no Pissarro, there might have been no Cézanne. Pissarro cleaned up his friend's palette and gave him light.

The importance of Pissarro's influence upon Cézanne's work with the palette knife was enormous and can be felt in all Cézanne's later landscapes. The instrument itself forced him to give up details and to work at synthesis, but it also demanded a no-less-important operation, that of 'seeing', that is, mentally choosing the part of the landscape to portray with the knife.

The tonality of this painting has not yet achieved the luminosity and vibration of Cézanne's better-known works. The greens do not have the brilliance that they were to have later, the characteristic blue contours have not yet appeared, especially in the shadows. For the foliage, the palette knife

Paul Cézanne: 'The Pond at Soeurs à Osny' (1875-7), 55 × 71cm. Courtauld Institute Galleries, London.

was held on its side at a 45-degree angle and the colour came from a blend of green earth and emerald green, or of emerald green and a little yellow ochre.

The light greens of the trees in the sunlight have as a base a sombre green to which a little yellow ochre and white have been added. For the leaves in the shadows, a little burnt umber was mixed in, especially for those parts in the upper right of the painting. The colours of the tree trunks were achieved by mixing burnt sienna with white and adding a little of the green of the darker foliage. For the darkest part of the trunks, the colour was augmented with dark green.

Enjoy yourself now as you choose your colours, spreading them with your palette knife on a sheet of paper to see what results you get.

Understanding the palettes of the great painters is one of the most exciting and important things you will learn about painting.

INDEX
Note: Numbers in italic refer to illustrations